D1526275

THE COMPLETE GUIDE TO UPLAND BIRD TAXIDERMY

THE COMPLETE GUIDE TO UPLAND BIRD TAXIDERMY

How to Prepare and Preserve Pheasants, Grouse, Quail, and Other Gamebirds

Todd Triplett

The Lyons Press
Guilford, Connecticut
An imprint of The Globe Pequot Press

The Lyons Press is an imprint of The Globe Pequot Press.

Printed in the United States of America

10 9 8 7 6 5 4 3 2 1

Library of Congress Cataloging-in-Publication Data

Triplett, Todd.
  The complete guide to upland bird taxidermy : how to prepare and
preserve pheasants, grouse, quail, and other gamebirds / Todd
Triplett.
     p. cm.
  ISBN 1–59228–689–5
  1. Pheasants—Collection and preservation. 2. Grouse—Collection and
preservation. 3. Quails—Collection and preservation. 4. Taxidermy. I.
Title.
QL696.G27T75 2006
598.6'075'2—dc22
                                        2005016730

I dedicate this book to Megan, who without grumbling—at least not too much—has helped me anytime I've needed an extra hand during the compilation of my taxidermy books. She brings a smile to everyone around her.

Game you yourself have gotten . . . is food for the soul. In it are the sights, the sounds, and the smells of a landscape, the weather of a day, the companionship of a friend, your rapport with the dogs and theirs with each other, the moment when their ranging bells suddenly fall silent as they freeze on point, the memory of the rush of your blood as you walk in to make the flush and the heart-stopping instant when the bird bursts from cover and towers, the shot, the puff of feathers on the air, and, yes, that ineffable moment, compounded in equal parts of self-satisfaction and self-reproach, when the dog brings it to you and you hold in your hand the creature you both love and love to kill.

—William Humphrey, *Birds of a Feather*

Contents

Preface

This September morning finds me perched in a medium red oak tree, overlooking a hardwood hillside in the mountains of North Carolina. The reason for my vigil will be obvious to anyone who yearns for those first few chilly mornings that signal the onset of harvest season. I was hunting white-tailed deer.

What do whitetails have to do with upland bird taxidermy, you may ask? Well, nothing and everything. (Confused? Just wait until you begin your first taxidermy project!) Hunting whitetails was my first love in the outdoors, the primary reason I began taxidermy, and to write and to look for a way to make my living in the hunting world. Had I not been drawn toward taxidermy for whitetails, I probably wouldn't have found one of the most pleasurable forms of taxidermy—mounting upland birds.

Many taxidermists prefer to work only on certain critters, with big game species easily the most popular. But these taxidermists are missing out on a fascinating aspect of their craft. The fact is, other than size, a deer is a deer, a bear a bear, and so on. But in the bird kingdom the common notion is: too many species, too little time. Birds are beautiful, colorful, unique, and easy to mount. Yes, I said birds are "easy" to work with. Most are small, so they aren't back-breaking to lug around, and their thin skins are easy to flesh and preserve. And the relatively small size translates to a lower cost for materials.

All in all, a bird is a great way to begin a taxidermy hobby or career, and it may lead you to a wider range of projects throughout the animal kingdom.

Introduction

T he Brittany slipped along the edge of a cut cornfield, nose high in the breeze. He cast back and forth until finally slowing as he caught some invisible scent. Cautiously he moved to a clump of brush overgrown with honeysuckle; then it was as if he just hit a wall. He stood frozen, with only his barely wiggling three-inch stub of a tail betraying the excitement within. I eased into position beside the dog as I listened to my step-grandfather softly deliver directions about how to finalize the deal.

I spoke quietly to the dog as I stepped past him, and he didn't move a muscle. I took another step, then another, before I heard that thrilling whir of wings. As the covey of quail came up, I swung on one of the trailing birds and the gun roared. Nothing. I had one more chance, and with the second shot the last brown and white bird in the group crashed to the ground. Right away, the dog went to work searching for the downed bird. It took only a few seconds for him to find and retrieve the little quail, and then he dropped it softly in my hand. I was ecstatic. I had my first bird on the wing and the dog work had been perfect. Little did I know at the time how truly great that little Brittany really was.

Just twelve years old, I had very little experience with birds or bird dogs. Sure, I had sat on the edge of a dove field and sky-busted, occasionally sniping a poor unsuspecting dove that happened to alight in a nearby tree, but my wingshooting skills were poor to say the least. Upland bird hunting over a pointing dog was a completely different experience, more difficult but

Upland bird hunting is a great way to get kids interested in wildlife and the outdoors.

also more exciting. And few things rival the sight of a fine bird dog working a covey of birds.

Since that first day I have ventured afield in pursuit of upland birds countless times. All those trips have been exciting, but in my mind's eye the dogs never seem to work as diligently or as smoothly as that little Brittany I shot my first bird over. I've forgotten many of the details of that hunt over two decades ago, but a few things are still crystal clear: the grandeur of a bird dog on point, the beauty of an upland bird in the air or in the hand, and the sheer enjoyment of being outdoors on a crisp fall day.

Hunting, in any form, is a rewarding and enjoyable activity, but there is something special about the camaraderie shared among upland bird hunters and their dogs. And the best way to preserve the joy of a great hunt is by preserving a bird from that hunt. It may be a child's first bird, a species you've been

A special bond develops between hunting partners and a working bird dog.

after for some time, or just the tangible result of time afield with a good friend.

Whether your goal is to take on a new challenging hobby, launch a career, or become a world-class taxidermist, I wish you the best of luck. Taxidermy is definitely an activity that will consume you, and it dovetails nicely with an interest in hunting. When I'm not in the field chasing game I still want to be talking about it, writing about it, or re-creating the experience by mounting wildlife taken during my outings. If you feel the same way, I think you'll find that upland bird taxidermy only adds to the pleasure you already take in hunting.

By carefully following the steps laid out in the pages ahead, you'll soon be creating your own wonderful and enduring works of art while preserving memories of days afield. The best initial advice I can impart is not to begin work right away. I know you probably can't wait to get started, or finished, with

The finished mount from a special hunt will provide a lifetime of memories.

that first taxidermy project, but it's important to first read a good portion of this book so you can familiarize yourself with terminology, techniques, dos and don'ts, the skinning process, fleshing and degreasing, and other elements of the mounting process. Then, after you have a solid understanding of what to expect, get your materials and proceed slowly, referring back to the text as needed. If you start this way, I guarantee you the initial stages will go more smoothly.

CHAPTER 1

Field Care

There is nothing more beautiful than a mature upland bird in prime condition that has been carefully mounted. A blue-ribbon pheasant or chukar is truly a sight to behold for hunters and non-hunters alike. And with practice, patience, and persistence, you will soon be able to put together such a project. But all of the knowledge and patience in the world can't create a beauty out of a mangled, poorly cared for mess.

Each year I have customers bring in some of these disasters. The hunter simply didn't understand the need for proper field care. In some cases, the unfortunate hunter thought the best thing to do as the bird lay flopping on the ground was to give it a final kick to the head to end its suffering. If it can be done to a dead bird or animal, I believe I have seen it. I guess the worst scenario I've ever been presented with was a pheasant that had been shot hard and then mouthed even harder by the retriever. Sometimes it's possible for the hunter to just wait for a better specimen, but many times the prize in hand is something particularly special that isn't easily replaced.

The poor care of game in the field doesn't stop there, though. I have taken in birds that started out in good condition before being shoved carelessly into the freezer. The result is often feathers bent and broken, heads broken off, and so on. Then there are the birds that didn't make it to the freezer for a couple of days for whatever reason.

A high quality mount starts with proper field care.

Many times, the hunter doesn't give a second thought to the condition of the bird until the taxidermist refuses to take in the horribly damaged critter or until he picks up a finished mount that doesn't look great.

The goal of any hunter who hopes to preserve the memory of a hunt or display wildlife in his home should be to end up with the most impressive mount possible. This always begins in the field with proper care of the bird and should continue throughout the mounting process. Even the most skilled taxidermist will have a tough time dealing with a poorly cared for bird. And trying to learn taxidermy on a poor specimen will be nothing short of a disaster. It has driven many budding taxidermists to the brink of quitting.

Other factors highlighting the importance of field care include the area in which you live and the area in which you have the opportunity to hunt. For example, pheasants are plentiful in the Midwest, but if you live in the South or Northeast these beautiful birds aren't readily available in the wild. You must make a lengthy trip to hunt wild birds or visit a preserve for planted birds. This is also true for many upland gamebird species across the continent. Chukar are generally located in the Great Basin region out west, woodcock in the eastern half of the country, and species like sage grouse are tied to habitat in the intermountain west. Some species, like ruffed grouse, have a wider range, but there are still many areas where this bird doesn't exist. So if you are far from home and only have a few chances at taking that bird of a lifetime, field care becomes vital.

Proper field care actually begins with proper preparation and planning before a harvest even takes place. In most cases, the hunter knows before venturing afield that he wants to preserve a special bird. Step one is having at least a general idea of the pose in which you'd most like to mount the bird and where you'd like to display it. This helps you select a bird that best matches these parameters.

Give some thought to how you want to mount your trophy before even pulling the trigger.

Suppose you know you want to mount a pheasant, and on a successful morning you take a limit of roosters. If you want to mount a bird in a flying pose, you should closely examine the back feathers of each bird, along with the tail and wing feathers, as these will be prominently displayed. If major damage has been done to a wing or tail on a particular bird, you may want to opt for another. If you prefer a standing mount, a few broken wing feathers can be hidden, but the breast, back, and neck feathers are of utmost importance. And with a pheasant, the tail is often considered the most critical aspect of a perfect mount.

Simple rules for bringing home a prime taxidermy candidate include avoiding or limiting feather loss, keeping the plumage free of any fluids (including water or body fluids), and cooling the bird down as soon as possible. It's not always easy to follow these guidelines in the field, but for the hunter/taxidermist the techniques become second nature and require very little effort and thought.

Avoiding feather loss is often tricky because of the ounce or two of lead shot that is sprayed at the bird as it flushes. A well-placed shot at a pheasant within twenty yards or so can wreak havoc on an otherwise perfect bird, but you can take precautions that minimize the damage. Although it is sometimes tough to keep your wits about you when a covey of quail rises or a pheasant bursts from cover with a loud cackle, knowing what you need to do beforehand will help you make a clean kill without destroying the carcass.

To prevent major feather loss, try not to shoot birds that are too close. This isn't always a problem, of course, as heavily hunted birds often flush wild as soon as they realize danger is nearby. But with lightly hunted birds or those from a preserve, you may literally have to kick them from the cover. The best distance is usually thirty to forty yards, as most shotgun patterns are wide enough at that point to avoid a solid, tight hit with the bulk of the pellets. If a special or seldom-bagged bird happens to get hit extra hard it often can be repaired, but such repairs are time-consuming and the results are usually less than stellar.

Although you will wash the bird prior to the mounting process, it is best to maintain a completely dry trophy in the field. Wetness is a major factor in unwanted bacteria growth, and blood and other body fluids contain proteins that are tough to completely remove without chemicals or harsh washing. To avoid getting blood on the feathers, carry cotton swabs in your shooting jacket and plug every orifice of the dead bird. This includes the mouth, anus, and any major shot holes. If the bird is bleeding lightly it's a good idea to clean the area with a paper towel.

No matter how well prepared you are, certain circumstances are often unavoidable. Some upland species are closely associated with waterways and may flush over open water, or you may be caught in a sudden rain shower. When a wet bird is something that can't be avoided, just pat it as dry as possible

Dispatch a wounded bird quickly and humanely, but without ruining feathers or tearing the skin.

with a clean towel before moving on to the rest of your field-care procedures.

One key area that has long been neglected by otherwise knowledgeable sportsmen is getting that bird in a freezer as quickly as possible. Many birds have higher body temperatures than other types of game, and heat and moisture are the primary ingredients for bacteria growth, which is enemy number one to the taxidermist. Even an otherwise properly cared for bird with very few damaged feathers can be lost due to slippage from bacteria buildup.

So if you've just taken a special bird that you've been after for some time, it may be best to head back to the truck and get the specimen to a refrigerator or freezer as soon as possible. If you are hunting in frigid weather you may not need to sacrifice the rest of your day afield, but when there is any question about the safekeeping of your prize, get it to a cool, dry area as quickly as possible. If you're far from home and leaving the hunt is out of the question, you can keep a small chunk of dry ice in a cooler back at the truck. Put a layer of plastic over the dry ice, then wrap the bird in a towel and place it on top. This type of preparation will give you anywhere from several hours to several days—depending on the life of the dry ice—to finish the hunt.

One final rule is to skip field dressing your bird. I am usually fanatical about field dressing any type of game, but for a bird to be mounted this usually creates more problems than it solves. When you open up the bird in the field, it's just too difficult to control the blood and other fluids that quickly contaminate the feathers.

Once a bird is successfully harvested and proper field-care guidelines have been observed, you are almost finished. If you have time to start work immediately on the mount, by all means do so. If not, proper storage in a freezer is your next priority. Arrange an open space in the freezer. Then, if possible, place the head under one wing, which reduces the possibility of snapping a thin neck while handling the frozen bird later on.

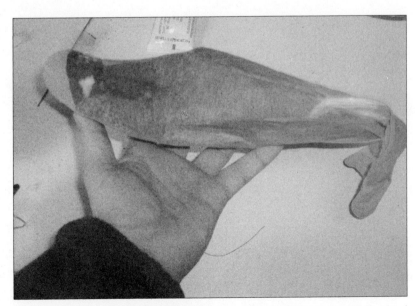

One method of minimizing feather loss or breakage is to insert the bird into the leg of an old pair of stockings.

You can also slide the bird one way into the leg of a pair of lady's hose to keep the feathers flowing smoothly in the proper direction. It can then be placed into a small plastic bag that will help prevent contaminants from getting on the feathers. Never put other items on top of the bird, even when completely frozen, as this could damage feathers.

Many upland gamebirds have medium to long tails, so pay close attention to this area. Place the bird on top of the freezer's other contents and carefully position the tail so it won't be crushed, or sandwich the tail between two thin pieces of cardboard and staple or tape them together. This should eliminate any undue damage to the tail feathers.

If you take the time to properly care for your future trophy in the field you will be rewarded with a bird that is a pleasure to work with and a higher-quality mount. If you don't, the frustrations that arise during your first attempt at the mounting process may lead you to throw in the towel before you even finish your first project.

CHAPTER 2

Reference and Anatomy

All my life I have been amazed with the beauty of wildlife. And I have always found the art that is derived from wildlife—paintings, sculptures, and taxidermy—fascinating. I used to think that there was some kind of secret or magic behind all of these trades. As a youngster I attempted to draw or paint wildlife scenes that were in my mind. Unfortunately, my work never measured up to my imagination. How, I wondered, could anyone know a subject so intimately that he or she could re-create it naturally in another form. Then, during my first trip to Yellowstone National Park the summer before I began my taxidermy career, I found a major part of the answer.

I had always wanted to visit this extraordinary place, so full of wildlife and majestic scenery. I spent most of my time studying, photographing, and simply enjoying the abundant wildlife. At midday, when many of the animals retreated to shade and privacy, I visited some of the natural wonders and exhibits.

Inside one of the information centers I found an artist painting an exceptional portrait of a buffalo. He did his "magic" right there in front of a crowd, creating flawless lines, shapes, and shadows seemingly without effort. I watched closely and began to notice that the artist would peer regularly through a small eyepiece on his workbench. After I observed him looking through this eyepiece several times I finally asked what he was looking at and why. He graciously offered me a look. I bent down and saw a photograph of a buffalo identical to the one being painted. Somewhat confused, I asked why he was constantly checking the photo. That's when he explained that all artists use reference material to help with anatomy, size, and other important features of their intended work. The secret to realistic re-creation was revealed, and this same rule of reference applies to taxidermy.

When I began learning the art of taxidermy I had been told something about using reference material, but without that experience in Yellowstone I might not have taken it as seriously. Without reference material, wildlife reproductions might look more like cartoon characters than living creatures. The best taxidermists in the world constantly study and observe the species they intend to re-create. Some even raise specific species themselves and keep live specimens nearby so they can observe every aspect of their anatomy and behavior. Even a taxidermist who has competed in world taxidermy championships and mounted hundreds, if not thousands, of upland birds will still constantly study and rely on his reference material for accurate re-creations. It's a never-ending process.

Reference materials are either 2-D, which includes photographs and videos, or 3-D, which includes death masks and live specimens. All types of reference are invaluable when preparing a mount, so don't rely on just one form.

Never use another taxidermist's mounted birds as reference. It is fine to study another's work. It's even recommended, as this may help you improve on a specific technique. But a mount is that particular taxidermist's idea of what a creature should look like. It will never be a perfectly accurate rendition of a live bird because it's colored by that individual's perception of the species. A live specimen is always the best reference, although it's not always possible to obtain or convenient to keep around.

Studying photographs and live birds will improve your ability to position your trophy naturally.

To study properly, you must first obtain a range of good reference materials. With the exception of live birds, these materials are relatively cheap and easy to acquire. If you don't think that a reference source is readily available, just look under your nose. Anyone who wants to mount his or her own upland birds is likely an avid hunter. And most serious hunters I know have stacks of old hunting magazines lying around.

Specialty magazines that often have great photos of live upland birds include *Gun Dog* and *Pointing Dog Journal,* both of which are devoted to hunting dogs and gamebirds. General hunting and outdoor magazines also will have upland bird photos occasionally, as well, and it pays to flip through them and mark or cut out useful photos. The best thing about magazine photos is that they are often shown in full color, and the supply is nearly endless—and free if you're pouring through piles of old periodicals you were planning to throw out eventually.

If you need specialized or more precise pictures, a full selection is available at most taxidermy suppliers. These photos are typically high-quality close-ups of individual areas on a particular species. I highly recommend getting at least one booklet for each species you plan to work with. For the best quality, get these from images from a qualified reference photographer.

An ideal way to begin a reference library is to set up folders for each species of interest. One folder might contain pheasants in all positions—flying, walking, standing, etc.—another might be for ruffed grouse, and another for quail, and so on until all the upland bird species are covered. Once you have sorted through your old magazines, you can keep current by sifting back through and cutting pertinent images from each new magazine you finish reading. This will serve two purposes. It will offer you lifelong reference material and it will make amends

Sporting magazines are a great source of inexpensive reference photos.

with a less than understanding spouse, who can't understand why so many magazines are just lying around.

As I mentioned above, the ultimate reference is a live bird. In an ideal situation the taxidermist would have ready access to an aviary for reference study. This is easily accomplished with upland birds. As long as you don't live in the middle of a city or have strict county codes that prohibit this type of animal ownership, you can just string a high fence with a top and purchase a few birds. Keeping a few different species can be entertaining as well as educational. Fortunately, pen-raised upland birds are relatively inexpensive and simple to raise.

If a personal aviary is out of the question, there are other options. First, you can draw from your own hunting experiences. Once you familiarize yourself with what to look for it is amazing what you will notice when watching wildlife. Though most encounters with wild upland birds are fleeting and at a distance, always take advantage of any opportunities to observe

The chukar is a popular pen-raised species, although wild birds are available to hunters in the Great Basin region out west.

birds up close. It is amazing what can be learned by simply watching a bird without disturbing it. Noticing something as simple as how the body of a bird shifts slightly while it walks or how its body contorts while scratching may help you re-create that natural movement in your mount.

In the initial description of reference material I noted that a good 3-D reference is the death mask. Though an upland bird taxidermist may have a difficult time acquiring this type of reference, there is a way to do so. But first you need to have a basic understanding of what a death mask is and how it is made. A death mask is a reproduction of a specific part of an animal's anatomy. For example, death masks are often made of the noses and eyes (the entire area around the eye) of big game animals, as well as their entire faces with muscle detail. Making a mold of a particular body part is used very little, if at all, among bird taxidermists, with the possible exception of a head cast to study how the eyes sit in the head or how the ear canals sit in relation to the eyes.

Occasionally a taxidermist will use a whole carcass as a 3-D reference. This practice is most common among competition taxidermists, but it can be very beneficial to the learning taxidermist, as well. Pluck every feather from a bird carcass that is otherwise in good condition—no broken bones and no major damage—and leave every body part intact. This will allow you to study the underlying structure without the mass of feathers getting in the way.

Pose the carcass in various positions. Notice how each body part works in relation to the rest: extend the wings, close them, bend the legs, straighten them, and so on. Completing this type of reference can be time-consuming and it renders the bird useless for any other purpose, so you will probably want to keep it in good condition by placing it back in the freezer after each use. You should be able to thaw and use the carcass for reference three or four times before having to discard it.

Once you've compiled a strong set of reference material, you will be ready to start learning how to read this roadmap to a lifelike mount. To better understand reference you must first understand a human's inclinations when viewing a picture. If you show someone untrained in reading reference a picture of a pheasant standing in a cornfield and ask them what they see, they will likely respond, "A bird." If they are slightly more observant, they may say, "A bird in a cornfield" or even "A pheasant," but that is usually as far as they go.

These answers are all correct, of course, but they don't cover what a taxidermist must take note of when viewing the same photo. Ask the same question of someone trained to view and understand reference, and they will likely respond with comments about the attitude of the bird (e.g., alarmed, resting, or feeding). They may mention an unruly feather on the back, head, or side, or they may notice the head position or a host of other minute details. Trained observers see elements far beyond the average person.

To do a competent job as a taxidermist you must break down a picture while studying it. Instead of looking at the image as a whole, you must learn to notice each detail of a much smaller area. An excellent way to train yourself to do this is to place a piece of paper with a small square cut in it over the photo. The size of the box will depend on the size of the photo you are working with; smaller is usually better, as you want to focus on each specific area before moving on.

Let's use a picture of a pheasant or other upland bird that is in a relaxed, standing position. Separate an individual area that you would like to learn more about, such as the wing area. Place your small box over this area and move a straight-edge horizontally or vertically across the opening. You will quickly spot angles and shapes that were previously unnoticed, which will help you with the proper positioning of your final mount.

To better analyze a bird photograph, you must break it down and study each specific area of the body in minute detail.

Or try boxing off the head area of a flying grouse. You should immediately notice the angle of the head to the neck, then the angle of the neck as it enters the body, the degree of turn in the head in relation to the body, and on and on. The straightedge will help you focus in on the smallest angles by giving you a clean line for comparison. The uses for the cutout and ruler are limitless, and they're very helpful for anyone trying to learn the art of close observation.

As a taxidermist your goal should be to "perfectly" duplicate the specimen you happen to be re-creating. This task is virtually impossible if you aren't intimately familiar with your chosen species. As your experience grows, so will your taxidermy skills and your ability to better understand and interpret reference. And solid observation skills will lend themselves well to related fields of taxidermy if you choose to expand your work and continue in this discipline.

ANATOMY

Anatomy, for our purposes, is the specific structure of a given species. This includes the muscular and skeletal structure of each upland gamebird. You may think that this subject is best left to sculptors and artists, but understanding anatomy is crucial for the aspiring taxidermist. It is true that today's manikins already possess the bulk of the necessary skeletal and muscular reproduction for gamebird taxidermy, but who's to say the sculptor didn't make a mistake? You, if you've studied enough anatomy and checked enough reference material. Besides, learning as much as possible about a subject will always help you re-create it more naturally.

How would it look if you mounted a pheasant with a wing sticking from its back and a leg from its side? Although you probably won't make a mistake of this magnitude, you may, without a good understanding of anatomy, complete a project that is anatomically incorrect. You might only be off by a centimeter, but this can sometimes dramatically affect how lifelike your mount appears when complete.

In big game taxidermy, it is sometimes easier to get away with a less-than-perfect understanding of anatomy. This is because the manikins produced for big game already include the body, neck, head, and legs (for a life-sized mount). Bird taxidermists aren't so lucky. Usually, the only presculpted body part available for birds is the core, and sometimes even that is not available.

Even with a manikin, the taxidermist must still attach the legs and wings in the appropriate places at the appropriate angles and craft and attach the neck. All of these pieces must be wrapped with a filler to replace muscle tissue that was removed during the skinning and preparation process. Without proper knowledge of anatomy, you may put in more than was taken out, leaving you with an unnatural appearance.

In recent years, manikin sculptors have began making presculpted necks for birds. Some come already attached to the manikin, while others can be purchased separately. These are great in the right situation, but at times the actual neck of the bird being mounted may be a bit shorter or longer than the mass-produced version. A manufactured neck can be an excellent tool during the learning stage, but you may need to make your own necks for some species.

Anatomy isn't one of those subjects you can fully master with just a few hours of work, but once you understand the basics your learning curve will increase dramatically as you do more research and tackle more projects.

You can learn a lot about anatomy before and during the skinning process. While preparing to start skinning your bird, swivel and bend the wings, legs, and body to get a feel for the range of motion. For example, you will only be able to bend a wing so far before a ligament or muscle group stops the movement. After the muscles are removed, you will be able to flex the wing past this point, but it won't look natural. A good understanding of the range of motion for each body part will help you prevent major mistakes in positioning during the mounting process.

When you're actually doing the skinning, notice how each bone is attached to the next and how the muscles are attached to the bones. This is a never-ending process, and your knowledge will increase each time you skin a bird. I've been skinning animals and birds for taxidermy for many years, but I always learn something new with each project.

Make mental notes of how all the parts go together so you can begin to understand what is natural and what isn't. And that is what taxidermy is all about—natural duplication.

CHAPTER 3

The Right Tools for the Job

Ask any veteran taxidermist to prioritize the importance of various aspects in achieving the right look in a finished mount and he will likely tell you: (1) tools; (2) reference; and (3) training and practice. Many novice taxidermists fail early in their attempts to learn the art of taxidermy because they are afraid to invest in the required tools, much less the luxury tools that aren't absolutely necessary but which shorten working time and produce better results.

Needless to say, the outcome of your efforts will be much more desirable, and the process more enjoyable, when you use the appropriate tools for each job. Some tools of the taxidermy trade may seem a bit pricey, but in the long run they are worth their weight in gold. Particularly in the initial learning stages, good tools make certain tasks much easier, and this in turn fuels your confidence and motivation to continue with the project.

The following is a description of the most common taxidermy tools, what their duties are, and whether I consider them optional for the beginner.

Latex Surgical Gloves. I know many taxidermists who neglect to use gloves of any kind while handling birds and mammals to be mounted. Their reason for being so careless is usually, "I can't feel my work as well with gloves on." In my opinion, an opinion shared by everyone who has seen firsthand the devastating effect of not wearing protective gear, this is without doubt a health bomb waiting to go off.

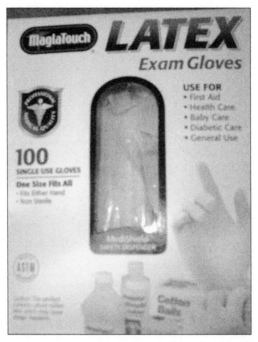

Latex gloves prevent any possible disease transmission.

Knives can be used for many taxidermy tasks, but scalpels are razor sharp, disposable, and sit nicely in your hand when attached to a balanced handle.

When it comes to the issue of gloves, the only question should be, "What size do I need?" Latex gloves are definitely not optional.

While most diseases prevalent in the animal kingdom can't be passed to humans, some can. Rabies is probably at the top of the list. I know many taxidermists who won't even accept raccoons or foxes for mounting. Though the chances of ever coming in contact with a bird or animal that has a transmittable disease is slim, once it occurs it's too late to consider the options. I have grown so accustomed to wearing latex gloves that the practice has spilled over into other areas: changing my vehicle's oil, painting, cleaning with commercial products, cleaning fish, and any other activity where my hands are exposed to dirt, strong smells, or harsh chemicals. After the chore is complete, I simply remove the latex gloves and lightly wash my hands.

Most taxidermy suppliers offer latex gloves in bulk, but the best place to obtain them is direct from a pharmaceutical company or a large retail store.

Scalpel. This is probably the most-used tool in the taxidermy trade. The scalpel's duties should be obvious: It is used to skin all birds and mammals. And while many taxidermists insist on a knife for skinning, buying scalpels negates the need for regular sharpening, and they are cheap when you factor in the time it takes to sharpen and resharpen a knife blade. Also, scalpels are much sharper than any blade sharpened by hand.

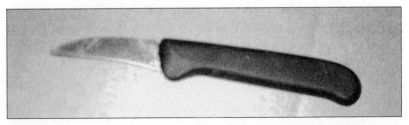

If you decide to go with a knife, choose one with a small fixed blade that will allow easy control of your cutting strokes.

Some taxidermists even believe that scalpels are *too* sharp, but once you learn to use them correctly your work will progress much more quickly.

Scalpels can be used alone, although they are best suited for attachment to a scalpel handle. You can buy small plastic scalpel handles, but I would advise that you invest the extra couple of dollars in a weighted, stainless steel handle. The weight helps the scalpel sit nicely in one hand while work is performed, and this type of handle will last a lifetime.

Be extra cautious when using scalpels. Even the poorest grades are razor-sharp, and if you make a careless slip you may end up with stitches to remind you of this fact. Scalpels are optional, but keep in mind that they are much more effective than a knife.

Most taxidermy suppliers carry scalpels, but blade companies typically offer the best prices. For taxidermy you only need non-sterile blades, which are much cheaper.

Scissors. Taxidermy scissors come in several different shapes and are designed to tackle specific jobs. But for most upland birds, you can get by with a small pair of scissors with slightly curved blades. These are very useful during the defatting process. Most species of upland bird—with the exception of turkeys—have very little fat, which can be removed quickly.

These small scissors are a great asset in removing the bulk of the fat before you take the bird to the wire wheel to finish up. Start this procedure slowly and carefully, as most bird skin is paper thin and easy to cut through. During the initial learning stages, err on the side of too much fat left on, rather than too little. As you gain experience, you'll learn to quickly trim off the right amount of fat and flesh without excessive damage to the skin.

Scissors are optional but highly recommended, and a good pair will save you a lot of frustration.

Bird Flesher. You probably won't need a bird flesher for most upland birds, as they have very little fat in comparison to waterfowl. Even this small amount of fat must be removed, of course, but you can often complete this task working by hand with a small pair of scissors. Nevertheless, you will need to learn how to use a bird flesher if you ever progress to mounting other birds—ducks, geese, turkeys—or any mammals. And depending on an individual bird's diet, you won't always be blessed with a pheasant skin that has no fat.

The bird flesher consists of a wire-wheel brush that rotates as the bird skin is lightly—very lightly—pressed against the wheel. This allows you to quickly remove large amounts of fat between each quill row, as well as around the base of each quill. If you aren't careful, you *will* tear holes in the skin, possibly to the point of rendering it unusable. I always recommend that beginners use the wheel sparingly. It can save you significant work time, but it takes practice and experience to master. Once you've been at it awhile, you'll be able to get a skin clean on the wheel with very little time or effort.

When purchased through a taxidermy supply company, these machines usually start at about $150 and go up from there. That is a lot of money for one tool, but a quality flesher will soon pay for itself with the reduced time it takes to de-fat a bird. If you plan to take up taxidermy as a hobby or occupation, I'd advise you to get a bird flesher. By the way, although the wire wheel was designed for birds it also lends itself well to small mammals.

If a factory-built flesher seems too expensive, it's possible for a beginning taxidermist to save a bit of money by assembling his own flesher. This is easily accomplished by salvaging a motor from a retired washing machine. These motors are usually still in good shape; the other components typically wear out first. It's important to understand that most of these motors

Most upland gamebirds don't require a flesher, but this machine will help with birds that have a thicker fat layer next to the skin.

have slightly more torque and turn at a higher rpm than a commercially made flesher, which makes it that much easier to damage the skin during the fleshing process. Again, it's mostly a matter of gaining experience behind the wheel, so to speak.

Attach the motor to a wooden frame, and then attach a motor arbor that will accept a soft wire-wheel brush. Finally, add a guard to block the fat and other debris flying off the wheel and you're in business.

Bondo is optional, but it's inexpensive and handy to have around.

Some taxidermists consider the wire flesher optional, especially for upland birds, as the bulk of the fleshing can be completed by hand, but I consider it a must-have item. Once you master it, you won't want to remove the fat any other way.

Bondo. It may seem a bit strange to find what is normally considered an automotive adhesive on this list of tools, but the fact is that without Bondo the taxidermy world would be scrambling for an exact substitute. Bondo has many uses in the taxidermy shop, including manikin repair, securing the base of a spread turkey tail, attaching artificial fish heads, attaching antlers to big game, and so on. No special formula is needed, any kind you find at a convenience store or automotive store will do.

Bondo is optional for upland bird taxidermy, but is useful in certain situations, such as when covering wires after attaching a mount to a driftwood base.

Wire. Wire is used to position an otherwise limp bird. Depending on the area being configured, you will need several sizes. Generally speaking, the wire gauge you need for upland birds ranges from about #8 for turkeys down to about #20 for most quail-sized birds. After you mount a couple of birds you may become comfortable with a different size, but the suggestions above are usually all you need.

Wire is not optional; without it you would have a floppy mess.

Bird Manikins. Many years ago, taxidermists had to wrap and shape their own bird bodies. This meant mashing and twisting handfuls of excelsior, otherwise known as wood wool, into the shape of the particular bird they were mounting. Once they achieved the basic size and shape they wanted, they still had to wrap twine around the mass to help hold everything in place.

Taxidermists also used soft foam manikins, which were carved into the proper shape using patterns from the exact bird body that was removed from the skin. This method and the old-fashioned wrapped body often resulted in more precise

Wire helps you position the bird—both internally and externally.

shapes, but these days it's difficult to justify the time and effort required.

As taxidermy began to catch up with modern methods, top taxidermists around the country began studying birds closely and taking very accurate measurements. After casting, measuring, and studying thousands of specimens, they began producing commercial bird manikins. Bird manikins consist of the same hard foam found in all mammal manikins, but they resemble a bird carcass almost exactly.

These manikins are highly recommended, especially if you're just starting out or are trying to make a living at taxidermy. They are usually anatomically accurate and hold wire well, and most have the wing and leg wire positions premarked. This is very helpful because a deviation of just a fraction of an inch in wing position can ruin an otherwise excellent mount.

Still, the art of wrapping and carving bodies is alive and well, and if you plan to practice bird taxidermy seriously you should learn this important procedure at some point. It can be the only alternative when you encounter a unique or oddly

Commercial bird manikins make life easier for the amateur taxidermist.

shaped bird for which a commercially made manikin isn't available. World-champion taxidermists continue to create their bird bodies this way, as they can be shaped more precisely for competition-quality mounts.

Although manikins may be considered optional, they are tremendous time-savers, particularly for beginners. There are plenty of other tasks to master in the early learning stages of taxidermy, so there is no sense trying to wrap your own bodies if you don't have to.

Degreaser. Proper degreasing is important when dealing with any fatty bird or animal. As stated above, upland birds don't usually have too much fat. But a quality degreaser still cleans the feathers, frees the skin of other oils, and produces a luster that enhances the finished mount. If you leave a little extra flesh and fat on the skin during the fleshing stage, which is a good idea when you're just starting out, a quality degreaser will save you. It will remove nearly all fats left behind, yet it won't damage the skin.

A quality degreaser can spell the difference between a beautiful mount and one with dull, lifeless feathers.

There are several methods for proper degreasing. Many top taxidermists swear by Dawn dishwashing liquid, claiming it is the only degreaser they use. I have used Dawn alone in the past, but I now prefer to use it in conjunction with a commercial degreaser. I've found that with a commercial degreaser my birds feel much cleaner, dry faster, and are much shinier.

Another alternative, one used by many very knowledgeable taxidermists, is Coleman fuel. Use extreme caution if you go this route, because this fuel is highly flammable. I have used Coleman fuel for degreasing purposes now and then. It is relatively inexpensive compared to commercial degreasers, very effective, and readily available. The primary disadvantage is that it can be so dangerous. A taxidermist must take extra precautions when using fuel as a degreaser, such as providing plenty of ventilation and keeping all sparks and heat sources well away from the work area.

I recommend that beginners stick with a commercial degreaser. Wait until you've gained some experience before trying

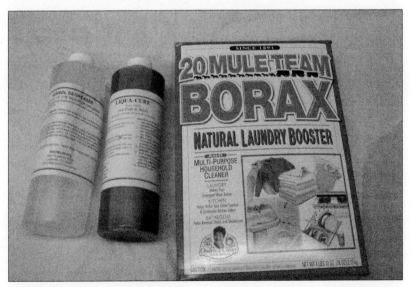

Dry preservative is probably the best choice for beginners, although some of the best taxidermists in the world also use it.

Coleman fuel. A degreaser could be considered optional for upland birds, but it will only enhance your mounts.

Dry Preservative or Bird Tan. A quality dry preservative or bird tan will help ensure that no bugs eat away at your creation. Most world-class bird taxidermists use dry preservative because it is quick and easy, but some recent bird tans now work just as fast. It's a personal choice, but for the beginner dry preservative is probably the way to go. It is easy to apply and includes no special mixes. And it's very easy to find; you can buy Borax, which works just fine on skins, at most grocery stores. If you are the experimental type, try different forms of preservation after you have completed your first few mounts.

Tumbler. This is definitely the big-ticket item on my supply list and, thankfully, it's also the only truly optional one. Don't take "optional" to mean not useful, though. A tumbler is a definite asset, but you can get by without one until you decide that taxidermy is something you'd like to continue with.

You can get by without a tumbler, but using it will reduce the workload and help you achieve a better finished product.

More than anything, the tumbler is a time-saver. Some wet birds can be given a short cycle in the tumbler and come out virtually dry, with only a slight touch-up needed before continuing the mounting procedure. The action of the tumbler also polishes the feathers, which enhances their luster.

Many taxidermists add things like corn cob grit or hardwood sawdust to the tumbler to condition the feathers, but for birds only corn cob grit should be used. Corn cob grit comes in two sizes: coarse and fine. A 50/50 mix of the two sizes is usually recommended for most birds, from the smallest to the largest. The tumbler can be filled from one-third to almost half full with this mix. Some other popular additives are odorless mineral spirits, dry preservative, or both.

Tumblers work well for cleaning and drying birds, and they also do a good job on mammal skins. So if you plan to make a longtime hobby of taxidermy, branching out from birds into mammals at some point, the tumbler will be a good investment.

Tumblers generally cost over three hundred dollars, depending on the size of the barrel and motor. If you aren't ready to make that kind of investment you can convert an old dryer for this purpose or simply place a small amount of tumbling medium into a large, thick-walled trash bag, add the bird skin, make sure there is a small amount of air to allow the contents to shift slowly from side to side, and then shake the bag for several minutes at a time until the feathers appear dry. These alternatives aren't as fast or effective as the tumbler, but they do work. The tumbler is optional, but if you're going to mount more than one or two birds it's a good investment.

Hair Dryer. The hair dryer is listed here because you might want to purchase one solely for your new hobby. Tumbling usually gets the bird 80-percent dry, so a hair dryer is useful for quickly drying spots that weren't finished, removing excess grit, and fluffing the feathers and down. Although there is nothing wrong with using your wife's hair dryer on birds, the lady of the house may object. You can use this opportunity to score some points, though. Buy a new hair dryer and give it to your significant other as a gift. Then add the old one to your taxidermy tool box.

Because heat isn't really necessary, I would recommend acquiring a hair dryer that has an optional heat switch. You don't want to get a bird too hot because this may promote bacteria growth and slippage. Commercial bird blowers that drive large amounts of room temperature air are also available. They are very handy but much more expensive.

Some kind of air blower is mandatory.

Regulator Needle. Regulator needles come in various lengths, and the longer ones are best for bird taxidermy. They can be used for everything from positioning feather tracts for pinning to layering individual feather rows or individual feathers. Regulators are inexpensive so you may want to buy several. This item is optional but very useful.

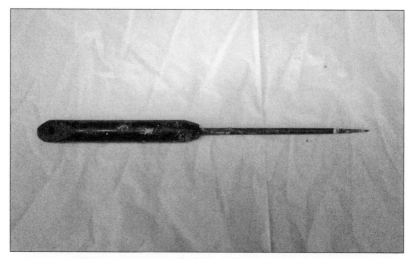

A regulator needle has many uses, from positioning the skin to properly layering individual feather tracts.

Neck Material. Initially, you may want to purchase manu-factured necks that attach nicely to commercial bird bodies. These preshaped necks take all the guesswork out of anatomy so you can concentrate on the basics. Neck material can be purchased cheaply in lengths of five to ten feet, which allows you to experiment without fear of running short.

Neck material is not optional.

Polyfil or Cotton. Polyfil or cotton has several uses in bird taxidermy, and either material works just as well. You'll need it to wrap legs or wings to replace the muscle tissue that was re-moved. When using any type of filler, a good rule of thumb is to go light. You don't want a bird that looks like it's on steroids. Polyfil or cotton is optional, depending on personal techniques.

Liquid Preservative. While dry preservative or bird tan is effective on the skin, you will need liquid preservative and a syringe for injecting portions of the wing and feet. These are usually unskinned areas that have little or no muscle tissue. There are several types on the market, and I really don't have a

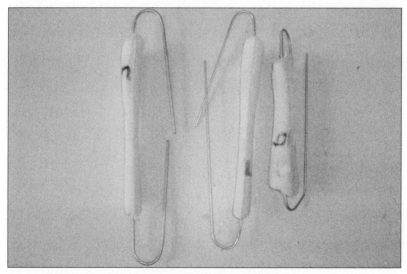

Presculpted necks are available for nearly every species.

consistent favorite. Many taxidermists like to use denatured alcohol, which is available at your local hardware store. Mix the denatured alcohol with an equal amount of water, and you're ready to go.

But be very careful when using any liquid preservative in a syringe. If you accidentally poke yourself in the hand it may become infected and will likely be quite uncomfortable for some time. Liquid preservative is not optional.

Airbrush. Preservation methods in the taxidermy industry have made tremendous advances, just like the techniques used to add the natural colors that bring the finished product to life. Not so long ago painting techniques involved paint brushes and automotive lacquers. Highly skilled taxidermists were able to achieve suitable results, but everyone else was left frustrated at the difficulty of doing even a passable job.

Upland birds don't need much finishing, so an airbrush is optional.

When taxidermists first began working with airbrushes, probably sometime in the 1980s, they were able to perform fantastic work. At about that same time, the paints used for taxidermy were also being refined. Instead of adapting paints intended for other uses, taxidermists began to specially formulate paints just for wildlife artistry. Today, an experienced hand can produce an incredible finished product, and beginners can shave months, if not years, off the learning curve.

The airbrush is helpful for replacing the diminished colors of the feet and legs (and occasionally the beaks) of birds. While it's technically optional, you'll find an airbrush and paint set well worth the minimal investment.

Miscellaneous Tools. This group includes ordinary tweezers for positioning unruly feathers, specialty needles and thread (dental floss will work in a pinch) for sewing incisions and holes, and brushes for cleaning up around fleshy areas or the eyes after the initial mounting process is complete.

Sculpting Tool. A sculpting tool is vital for shaping and sculpting the specimen throughout the mounting process. These are available in plastic or stainless steel versions. The stainless steel model costs a bit more, but if well cared for it will last a lifetime. This item is not optional, as every taxidermist should have a sculpting tool.

Artificial Eyes. Several brands of artificial eyes are available, and it really comes down to individual preference. Many taxidermists believe that the eyes are crucial for bringing a mount to life, and fortunately most on the market today are of good quality. I like flex eyes, primarily because they come with a presculpted eyelid, which helps to make a mount more convincing. For the appropriate size and color, consult a taxidermy supply catalog.

Videos and Classes. These may not seem like tools, but they provide an avenue of learning that will help the novice taxidermist master his trade or hobby much faster than a book alone. There is no substitute for actually seeing how a particular process is completed on video, and the hands-on experience gained in a class is invaluable.

Most taxidermy suppliers have an abundance of videos featuring well-known taxidermists doing what they do best. The subject material of these videos ranges from the smallest of birds to the largest of mammals, along with fish and reptiles and nearly every other animal that could possibly be preserved. Even the trained taxidermist will find these videos useful, as they present another perspective on the mounting process.

Obviously, videos and classes are optional, as you should be able to use this book and the appropriate amount of time and effort to complete your bird mount, but adding these elements to your training will certainly speed things up.

WHERE TO FIND TOOLS

A lot of the supplies covered in this chapter can be purchased through a local vendor, but at some point you will need to contact a taxidermy supplier. This is the only place you will be able to find some of the specialty equipment. One of the oldest taxidermy suppliers in the country is Van Dyke's. They have helped taxidermists worldwide begin their hobbies and, for some, their careers, and they have a vast assortment of nearly every type of taxidermy-related item available. Van Dyke's also offers its customers technical advice from an on-staff taxidermist. Such advice can be priceless. To order their catalog, call 1–800–843–3320, or visit their website at www.vandykestaxidermy.com. You can also use the Internet to find other excellent taxidermy suppliers.

CHAPTER 4

Skinning

Proper skinning of any bird or animal is a key ingredient in completing a quality mount. Most hunters have skinned quite a few birds in preparation for the grill or stovetop, but skinning for taxidermy obviously requires a much more delicate hand. It can make or break a hunter's trophy.

Several types of incision work well for skinning. The ventral incision is easily the most popular, and it's the one most often referred to throughout this book. I encourage you to experiment with other incisions like the side incision and back or dorsal incision, which can be useful in some situations. But most taxidermists, including me, rely on the ventral incision for almost every pose.

If you are starting with a fresh bird you're ready to start skinning. But if your trophy is stored in a freezer you must allow it time to thaw first, at least to the subsurface of the muscle tissue. This reduces tears in the skin, which are more likely when the skin remains frozen to the carcass. Proper thawing also makes the entire skinning job much easier. Upland birds aren't insulated as well as waterfowl or turkeys, but they can still take a full day or so to thaw. Even skins without the carcass that are unfleshed and unpreserved will likely take a bit longer to thaw than you realize.

Although skinning can be messy, do your best to maintain a clean, dry bird. This is particularly important with upland birds, because I like to skip the washing step if at all possible. (This only applies to birds with very little damage or ones that can be skinned and fleshed without soiling the feathers; realistically this is about one in ten.) During the initial learning stages, you should work through all the steps, washing included, so that you have a solid understanding of the entire process.

Start by preparing your work area. I have found that freezer paper or brown wrapping paper makes a great work surface. Pull a couple of lengths off the roll and tack them into place. Once the skinning job is complete, you can simply pull up the paper and throw it away. This removable paper isn't a must, but it is inexpensive and readily available. I also like to sprinkle a generous bed of dry preservative (Borax will work) on the paper before putting the bird down. This will soak up any excess fluids. Otherwise, you could be rolling the bird around in a terrible mess that might hinder the final product.

Once the skinning table is ready, make sure all the necessary tools are placed within easy reach. This is primarily for time management, as you will find things go much more

A clean work area is the first step in maintaining an undamaged skin.

smoothly when everything you need is right at hand. I keep an extra supply of dry preservative nearby to help soak up any body fluids that may seep onto dry feathers during the skinning process. Keeping your bird as clean and dry as possible before the washing process will pay huge dividends later on.

By the way, I recommend that you read through the entire text of this book before skinning your first taxidermy project, as you may want to add an extra step or two. For example, if you're not planning to mount the bird with an artificial neck it can be very helpful to take some measurements of the natural neck before skinning for reference later on. (This is less important if you're going to substitute an artificial neck.) You may also want to trace the wings and legs from side and back angles before skinning to have some kind of reference at hand if you need to rebuild these areas during the mounting process.

Ventral Incision

Place the bird on its back and locate the point of the breast bone, slightly more than midway up the body. This should be easy to find. Now locate the anal opening, which is near the base of the tail primaries. Once you've located both areas, separate the feathers along the breast with a regulator needle or thin piece of wire. Most upland birds have a narrow strip of open skin running down the center of the breast bone that becomes visible when the feathers are pulled apart. Use a scalpel or knife to cut smoothly from the high breast point to the anal opening. Then sprinkle the area with preservative to soak up any fluids that leak from the incision, as these may contaminate the feathers.

Start peeling back the skin. Just remember that some upland bird skins are easier to tear than others, so be careful. Doves, woodcock, and quail are probably the most tender,

Use a regulator needle or short length of wire to spread the feathers along the ridgeline of the breast.

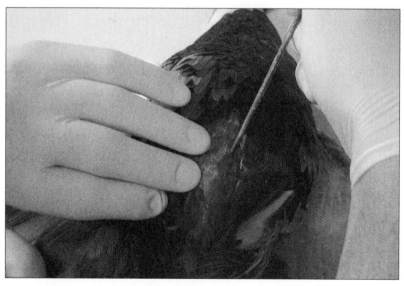

Cut carefully from the breast point to the anal opening. The skin is very thin, so it isn't necessary to go too deep.

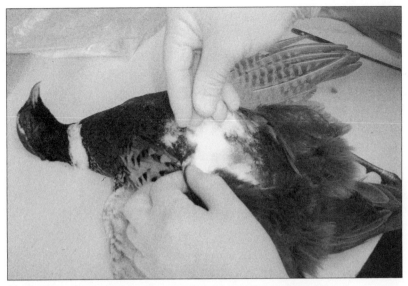

To prevent fluids from contaminating the feathers, sprinkle Borax or dry preservative on the breast incision and any fleshy areas.

Slowly peel the skin to each side, being careful not to lengthen the incision by tearing.

while pheasants, grouse, and chukar are typically a bit tougher. It is sometimes best to begin by pinching your way up one side at a time and then use the scalpel to work sections of skin free of the carcass. After you make a little progress you might have better success using only pressure from your hands to separate the skin from the body. This reduces the number of tears associated with overzealous application of the scalpel blade. Keep the scalpel handy for spots where the skin seems to be attached firmly to the underlying muscle tissue.

After the skin is free for a couple of inches on either side of the incision area, begin working your fingers between skin and carcass along either side of the body. You ultimately want the skin to be loose on both sides. Generously apply dry preservative between the loose skin and muscle tissue underneath. When you have the skin loose on each side almost to the back area, begin to work toward the thighs.

Start loosening the skin around the thigh. When the inside of the thigh is easily visible, cut slowly at the junction of the

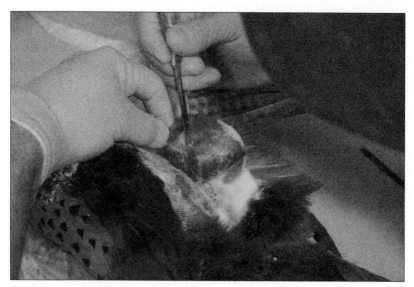

Work a finger along the thigh to free the knee area, femur, and tibia.

thigh and the drumstick (the thigh is properly called the femur and the drumstick the tibia). After severing this joint, continue to separate the skin from the thigh area, moving toward the back. Once severed, the tibia or lower leg should lie to the side, completely out of the way. This procedure may take some getting used to, so go very slowly at first. It's perfectly fine if you have to make several cuts before the joint is completely severed.

The most important consideration is not cutting through the skin. If you do make an unintentional cut it's probably repairable, but the finished product may suffer slightly and you'll have to do some extra work. It's much better to go slowly and carefully to avoid making tears in the first place.

When the joint on each leg is free, place each leg to the side of your bird. This will keep them out of the way and allow you to concentrate on loosening the skin along the sides down to the tail section. Continue working until you close in on the tail. Now free the skin slightly past the vent opening.

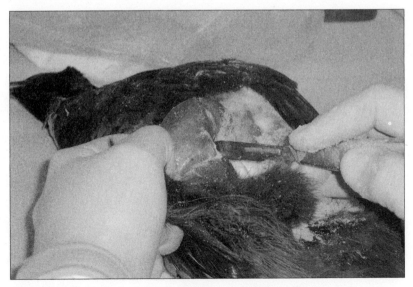

Cut slowly through the knee area without slicing any skin tissue.

Once the knee has been severed, it's possible to invert the lower leg for further fleshing. (This bird is a grouse, but skinning techniques are the same for all upland gamebirds.)

Begin to cautiously cut toward the back of the bird. The goal here is to sever the tail section and continue skinning down the back. This is best done by cutting through a joint of the tail.

With the tail severed, slowly and carefully work the skin up toward the front of the bird. I usually leave the bird on the working table until the skin is loose from the carcass, at least for a couple inches down the back. After that, it is often best to hang the bird, which makes the rest of the job easier.

Many taxidermists use a bird gambrel to hang the bird. The gambrel typically has three lightweight chains, approximately six to eight inches in length, attached to what looks like three large fishing hooks, one on each end. It's very simple to use. Just embed the three hooks into the rear area of the bird and attach the junction of the chains to a secure point just lower than shoulder height and continue skinning.

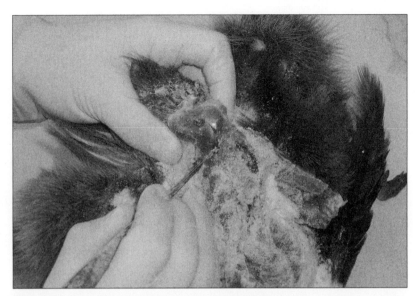

After the skin is free along each side of the body and to the anal opening, carefully cut through the base of the tail. Make the incision where the tail readily flexes at its attachment point to the body.

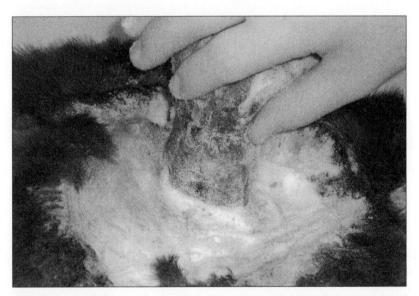

Continue to slowly work the skin free along the back for a couple of inches.

Another method for hanging birds is to take a length of 12-gauge wire, sharpen it at one end, and bend it into an "S" shape, so it appears to have a hook on each end. With the wire in the desired shape, push the sharpened end into the carcass above the thigh area and through the back.

No matter which method you choose, make sure the bird is secure by giving it a gentle tug. You don't want it to fall while you're working on it.

If the bird has been properly thawed the wings should droop slightly toward the floor. If not, carefully pull them down a bit. This will shift them forward, which should allow plenty of room for the skin to move until you reach the shoulder area. Loosen the skin farther along the back until you hit the shoulder blade. Sometimes the skin along the back is tough to separate with just your hands. If so, this is one of those times when you may find it easier to use a scalpel.

Continue loosening the skin toward the base of the neck until the connection between the wing bone and the body is

Now hang the bird and skin until you reach the wing area.

Cut just behind the base to sever the humerus bone—the upper portion of the wing being held between the thumb and index finger—from the carcass. If you go slowly it will be easy to find the ball-and-socket joint.

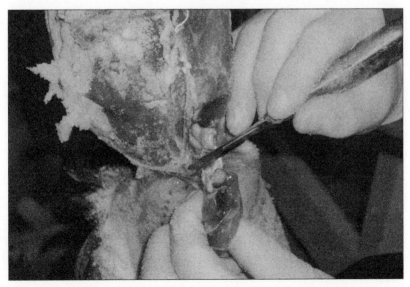

Notice the angle of the cut and the ball at the end of the humerus.

visible. Use a scalpel to cut the wing free from the body. After each wing bone is free it should fall out of the way. This allows the skin to invert, which makes the final skinning much easier.

From this point, it should be a simple matter to dust the skin area with some preservative (to ensure a good grip) and pull the skin toward the head area. Gently work the skin free of the carcass and continue along the neck. I try to skin all birds to the base of the head. Some upland birds can be skinned fully to the forward portion of the head (to the beak), while the heads of others must be severed at the base. In the latter case, an incision will be made underneath the head/neck junction to complete the skinning process.

Grouse and chukar can usually be fully skinned to the beak area, but you'll have to deal with other species bird by bird. To find out if you should attempt to fully skin the head, gently work the skin forward from the base of the skull with your

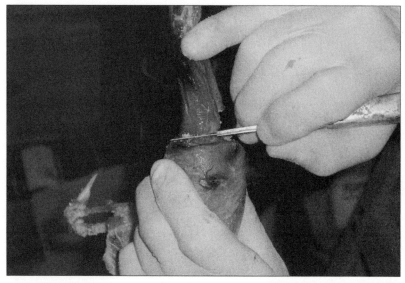

Sever the skull from the neck or, if possible, completely invert the skin across the skull.

fingers. If it inverts easily, you shouldn't have a problem. But if the skin seems excessively tight, you should stop and just sever the head at the head/neck junction with a pair of snips.

If the skin can be inverted, proceed slowly, using the scalpel very lightly to avoid cutting this tender skin. At the rear of the skull, you will notice an ear canal on each side. Cut slowly through both and continue working the skin toward the beak. The next sensitive area is around the eyes. Starting from behind the eye socket, continue to pull the skin forward while making very light cuts. Keep going until you see a small opening in the light membrane that surrounds the eye. Be careful to not cut the eyelid, as this extremely small area can be difficult, if not impossible, to repair. Experience is the best teacher, and with practice you will be able to finish this task with no problems. Until then, be patient and work slowly.

After skinning past each eye socket, free the skin slightly forward of that point and stop. Skinning is now complete, and the head can be severed at the base of the skull. These procedures remain the same whether you sever the head at the base of the neck first or completely invert the head. The only difference is that you must make an additional cut if you severed the head before inverting the skin. This extra cut is an incision under the neck and head that allows you to pull the head through it for a full cleaning. If you were able to completely invert the skin off the head, you can skip this step.

The leg and wing bones also must be inverted and the muscle tissue removed. I like to begin with the legs and wings, then finish by inverting and cleaning the head.

To remove the drumstick muscle, make sure the skin is free along almost the entire length of the tibia. This is best accomplished by holding the free end and slowly working the skin toward the scaled area of the lower leg. Several tendons attach the muscle to the tibia just above the joint where the feathers meet the skin. Sever these and use a knife to separate the leg muscle the entire length of the bone. The muscle tissue should now be attached to only the ball of the tibia. Clip the tibia adjacent to this ball, which will also sever any attached muscle tissue.

Now clean the inside of the bone by inserting a piece of wire into the leg bone. This forces out any unwanted blood or fat. Next, put a small amount of preservative into the opening and work it in with the wire to absorb any excess fats.

The procedure for the wing bone is very similar. Grip the ball of the wing bone and slowly separate the skin from the humerus, moving toward the elbow area. Now cut the muscle tissue free from the elbow to the shoulder end of the wing bone using clippers or a knife. When both sides are finished, pull the skin right side out again. Sometimes it may be helpful to wrap twine around the ball of the humerus/wing bone or the tibia/leg bone and hang the piece while skinning.

To invert and clean the skull, lay the head onto the top, or crown. Use a scalpel to cut a straight line along the underside

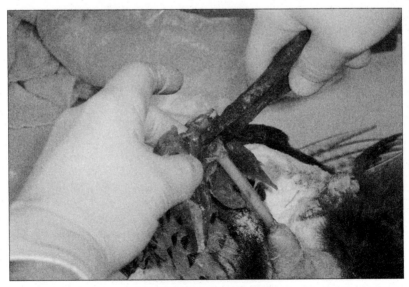

Cut toward the free end of the tibia to reach all the muscle tissue, and then remove the end of the tibia with a pair of wire cutters.

of the head, moving rearward from within a quarter inch of the mandible (beak). Make the cut just to the rear of the skull, or slightly farther if necessary. A longer cut may be required depending on the length of neck tissue that was left attached to the skull. Place a small amount of dry preservative along the incision, then begin to work the skin free on each side until the neck and head can be inverted.

Now use the scalpel to carefully free the skin toward the front of the head. The first obstacle you will encounter is the ear canal on each side. After cutting through the ear canal, continue skinning until you reach the eye area. This is a sensitive area, so proceed with caution. Start cutting slightly behind the eye opening, which will free the eyelid. Continue cutting until the skin is free just past the eyelids. Slightly beyond the eyelids is usually far enough.

To finish the preparation of the skull, you must remove the eyes, attached neck tissue, and the tongue, along with as

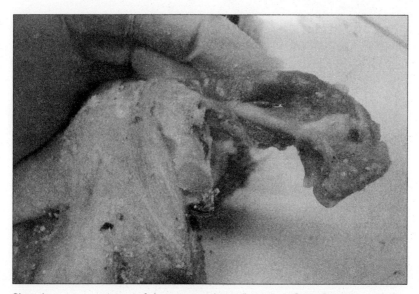

Skin the upper portion of the wing and cut the tissue free along its entirety. Clip or shape the ball so it will conform smoothly to the manikin.

Although it isn't recommended for beginners due to the delicate nature of the skin along the wing bones, the wing can be fully inverted and the muscle tissue removed for a seamless wing.

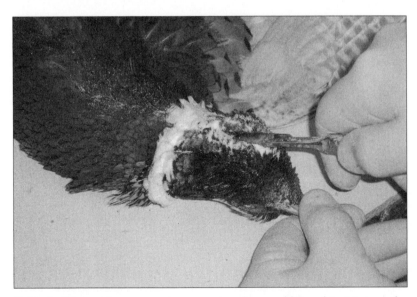

If the skull has to be removed you must make an additional incision on the underside of the head and neck. Sprinkle on some dry preservative, then make a cut of roughly one and a half inches from behind the beak to the rear of the skull.

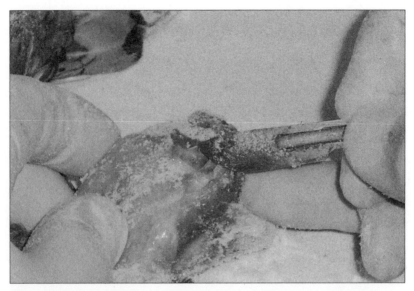

The ear canals are the first delicate areas you encounter on the head.

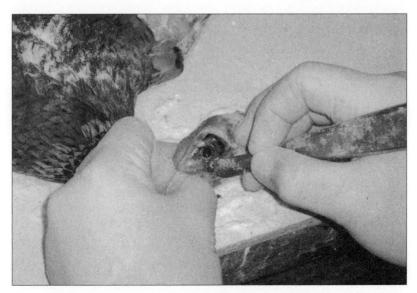

Cut carefully along the eye area because the actual diameter of the eye is much larger than just the portion you see before skinning.

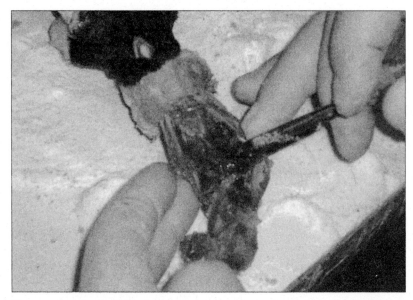

To prepare the skull for final mounting, remove the eyes, all flesh, and the tongue and clean the brain cavity.

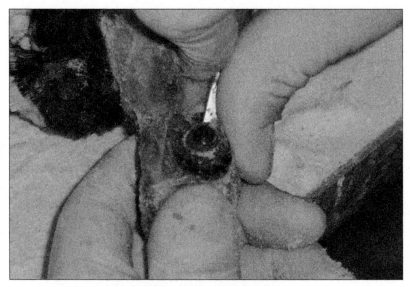

Work carefully when removing the eyes. If punctured, they will release a dark fluid that may stain the surrounding feathers.

much tissue as possible. The eyes are best removed with a sculpting tool or a specialized eye tool (available from most taxidermy suppliers). This is a delicate operation, because the eye will secrete a dark fluid if punctured. This fluid isn't harmful, but it can be very messy. Make a clean cut at the base of the skull to remove the neck tissue, and insert a sculpting tool into the brain cavity and remove the brain tissue. Once the bulk of the tissue is out, pack dry preservative into this opening. Finish by cutting along each side of the tongue area with the scalpel, then remove the tongue and any excess flesh.

At this point, you may continue with the fleshing and degreasing or place the skin in the freezer to work on later. If you store the skin for the time being, don't break or crush any feathers. I prefer to store my bird skins in a small bag on top of other items in the freezer.

CHAPTER 5

Fleshing and Degreasing

Birds are well adapted to their environment. They are typically able to endure the harshest weather winter can dish out. This is due to the great insulating properties of the feathers and feather down, in addition to a thin to heavy fat layer under the skin. Also, thanks to an oil gland situated above the base of the tail, a bird can remain dry in all but the heaviest rain. If you ever watch a wild or domestic bird for any length of time you will notice it placing its beak to this area and then grooming itself. This action cleans, waterproofs, and positions the feathers.

This protection is ideal while the bird is alive, but for the taxidermist, it can present problems like dull, lifeless feathers or grease leaching from a mount several years after completion. (The latter usually occurs more often with waterfowl, as they carry a lot more fat than upland gamebirds.)

In rare situations you will be able to get by without using a fleshing wheel or a degreaser, but early on you should always fully flesh the bird skin and then degrease it thoroughly. This provides extra insurance that the mount will be of the highest possible quality and eliminates all guesswork. Down the road, as your knowledge grows, you may bypass these procedures with some individual upland birds. But skipping the processes of fleshing and degreasing would only be an option with an especially lean bird, one with no blood on the feathers, and this would be predicated on your doing a very clean skinning job.

All the taxidermy techniques must be done properly to produce a quality mount, although some procedures carry a bit more weight than others. Fleshing and degreasing rank near the top of the list. If you slip and cut a couple of holes during skinning you can usually just sew them up. And if a feather tract shifts slightly during mounting it will probably go unnoticed to everyone except a trained taxidermist. But mount a bird with flat, dull, and lifeless feathers and even a child will notice.

Fortunately, proper fleshing and degreasing is a relatively simple procedure. As with the other steps, this isn't a race. Take your time and do it right. An experienced taxidermist can flesh a bird in less than twenty minutes, but it may take a beginner over an hour. Once the mount is complete, you will definitely be glad you spent the extra time on this step.

Fleshing incorporates the use of scissors, snips, and a fleshing wheel, and quality tools make a big difference. A fleshing wheel is a large investment, and you may be hesitant to spend so much on one tool early in your taxidermy work. But rest assured, whether your time in taxidermy is short or lasts a lifetime, you will never regret purchasing high-quality equipment. I thought I could get by without a fleshing wheel when I began my own career, but I soon learned the hard way just how important this item is.

If you're still not convinced, just look at the numbers. Most basic upland bird mounts cost roughly $200, but for a big bird like a wild turkey this cost may be more in the neighborhood of $500. Yet you can easily get by with spending around $200 for good equipment. So after completing just one basic bird mount, your equipment will essentially have paid for itself. Even if you spend $400 for equipment, you'll quickly recoup this investment with a couple of mounts. But if you are like many of the outdoorsmen I know, you will become addicted to wildlife artistry. And once this addiction takes hold, a couple of bird mounts will be a drop in the bucket.

There are a few things you need to understand before you begin the fleshing process. For one thing, clean feathers with properly fleshed roots are much easier to work with. Feather position is a good gauge for whether or not your fleshing has been done correctly. When the bird is fully mounted and completely dry, feather position should have changed very little from its original placement. When the skin is poorly fleshed the tissue surrounding the feather quills shrinks and shifts as it dries. And when this tissue shifts, so do the feathers. So it is important that each feather base be as free of tissue as possible.

FLESHING

Before starting, you must completely invert the bird skin. Simply reach through the incision already made, grasp the neck and head area, and pull it back through the incision. Be careful not to tear anything. Invert the legs and the wings as far as they will go, and you are ready to continue.

Fat attached to the skin is always an issue, but it varies depending on things like food availability, the bird's age, time of year, and other variables. A young bird taken early in the season before the weather gets too cold may have little, if any, fat. On the other hand, a mature bird taken during a severe winter may have a thick, tough fat layer.

Start fleshing with a pair of scissors or snips. Sprinkling the fatty tissue with a preservative will make the otherwise slick tissue easier to grip and pull free. At times, it's even possible to remove excess flesh with your fingers. But take care while doing this. Early in my career I grabbed hold of some muscle and fat tissue and began to pull. I somehow managed to pull several feathers completely through the skin. From then on I was very cautious about ripping any tissue from the skin. When in doubt, use scissors. Also, try to avoid cutting any feather

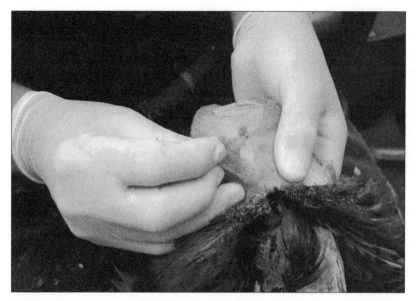

Apply a small amount of dry preservative and then slowly pull the flesh free, being careful not to draw feathers through the skin.

roots with the scissors, as this too will cause unwanted feather loss. Sometimes, depending on the individual bird, this pinching and pulling free of tissue and fat may be all that is required to completely de-fat the bird.

A pair of cutting pliers or snips can be very useful during the initial stages of fat removal. In particularly tough areas the pliers help you gain purchase on the fat area and the snips cut it free.

After the bulk of the fat is pulled free, it is time for the fleshing wheel. As mentioned earlier, this may be overkill on some upland gamebirds, but for others it is a great way to speedily remove large amounts of fat. I use a Van Dyke's Bird Flesher, which has earned a good reputation within the taxidermy business. It's a quality machine and is reasonably priced in comparison to most other fleshers.

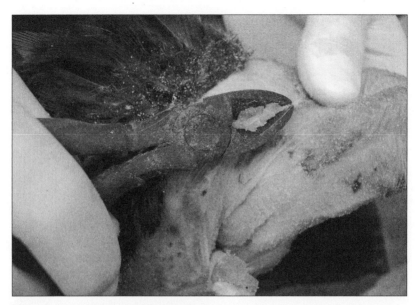

Pliers are handy for cutting away flesh.

After removing loose flesh around the base of the tail, cut slots between the quills to help reach these difficult areas.

I'd recommend buying one that has a motor large enough to "wheel" away the fat from even the toughest birds—like turkeys and geese, so you can eventually expand into other areas of taxidermy—but small enough that smaller skins won't be jerked from your hands and wrapped around the still-spinning brush. One-quarter horsepower is a good starting point. By the way, don't let the possibility of the skin getting wrapped around the brush scare you, because it happens to everyone, even the best taxidermists in the business. If you have a fleshing motor of the right size, the entangled skin will force it to slow significantly or stop, minimizing potential damage.

You can flesh a bird fast and thoroughly using a systematic method. It is best to start on the front of the bird and work your way back, and go from left to right as the brush turns clockwise. Moving this way throws the flesh onto the tail of the wire brush rather than into its path. If you work in the opposite direction you will eventually build up a large amount of fat in front of the working brush. It's a lot like a snowplow that

The fastest way to strip flesh from the skin is with a fleshing wheel.

accumulates snow in front of the blade. Eventually there will be too much to push. With the wire wheel, this slows progress and may cause burns or tears.

You will quickly find that most birds aren't made up of a mass of randomly placed feathers. Rather, there are usually several different feather tracts that are best worked on separately. I like to begin fleshing with the wing bones, then the leg bones, then the rest of the skin.

I start the body with the breast section, simply because it's the routine I've become comfortable with. Depending on the particular bird, some tracts will present more problems than others. The breast area is typically the fattiest. Once this area is complete, I continue with the back, scapulars, thigh area, and tail quills.

When you hold the inverted skin in your hands you can easily see a pattern to the feather quills. They stand out like rows of corn in a field; the smaller the bird, the smaller the rows and vice versa. This actually makes the fleshing process a

Removing flesh on the ends of exposed leg and wing bones is easier with a wheel.

bit easier. As you begin fleshing the body these rows will become wider and you should be able to place at least a portion of the wheel in between each one. After all the rows in a feather tract are clean, I turn the skin 90 degrees, keeping the feather quills lying in the approximate direction of the turning wheel, and continue wheeling away fat.

In the neck area the feathers are very close together so I go lightly across the top, wheeling away the bulk of the flesh. The same goes for the back area. These areas are probably the most fragile spots on the bird skin. Be very careful with this tender skin, as it's not hard to tear holes or make burns.

You may find it helpful to keep a bucket of water nearby when you're learning how to use the wheel. You can occasionally dip the skin if it starts to heat up from the friction of the wire wheel. Be patient. At first it may seem impossible to get good results, but stick with it and you'll quickly get a good feel for how much pressure is required to remove the unwanted flesh.

After a thorough job with the fleshing machine you will probably need to shift back to the scissors. Cut away any flesh that you weren't able to pull free with the wheel for fear of tearing a hole.

WASHING AND DEGREASING

With most of the visible fat and flesh removed, it is time to turn your attention to degreasing. A proper degreasing solution will yield beautiful oil-free feathers. Well-cleaned feathers have a shine matched only by those of a live bird. Again, after you gain some experience, you may want to skip these steps with certain upland birds, but I recommend that everyone complete them on the first few projects.

There are many methods for degreasing, but some are better than others. Degreasing should always begin with a bath, which eliminates excess blood, dirt, and other unwanted extras. The old standby for most taxidermists has long been Dawn dishwashing liquid. Fill a large tub with cool water and squeeze in a small amount of Dawn. Make certain the detergent mixes well with the water, and don't worry about using too much because you will shortly rinse out the excess.

Submerge the skin into the solution, and gently feel the wet feathers with your hands. You should be able to detect any clumps of blood or dirt that may be stuck to the feathers. Work large debris free with your fingers and switch to a small toothbrush for cleaning the wing feathers. Brush gently with the grain of the feather until the stain is removed. I like to grasp the wings and lightly work the skin back and forth and up and down. This loosens any additional unwanted particles. Then I just let the skin soak for about thirty minutes, depending on how dirty it was to start with.

After a good soak, I pull the skin from the bath and rinse the feathers thoroughly under a water source. Hold the skin

Dawn dishwashing liquid is one of the safest, simplest, and best degreasers for upland birds.

If any contaminants cling to the feathers, carefully massage the area until it is clean.

and allow the running water to completely penetrate the feathers. When the water running off turns clear, the bird should be rinsed thoroughly. Another effective means of rinsing is to place the skin into a fresh pail of water and then swirl it from side to side. A combination of the two rinsing methods ensures that all degreasers have been removed, which only enhances the workability of the skin and feathers during the mounting process. This also improves the overall appearance after the mount is finished and dry.

Many well-respected taxidermists move on at this point, even with the oiliest skins. Upland birds aren't usually too greasy, but I like to continue the cleaning process with products made specifically for degreasing. You'll see a variety of these in the taxidermy supply catalogs, and I'm not partial to any particular brand. Mix up enough of this commercial solution to resubmerge the skin, and let it soak for another thirty minutes or so. Always wear rubber gloves when working with a commercial degreaser. These chemicals are specifically designed to remove oil, so if you submerge your bare hands in the solution you may end up with a severe skin irritation.

In the chapter on tools, I also mentioned using Coleman fuel (gasoline is another substitute) for degreasing. Many taxidermists swear by this type of "gas bath," but due to the risk of fire or even an explosion I can't really recommend it to the novice. Even a tiny spark could ignite the concentrated fumes. If you plan to go this route it is best to do the job outside where there is plenty of air circulation. And wear protective gear like gloves, a mask, and an apron.

Specially made degreasers may cost a bit more than Coleman fuel, but the few extra dollars also provide piece of mind, and commercial degreasers are very effective. Of course, if you feel like the Dawn alone did a pretty good job removing grease from the skin, you may want to stop there. Just remember that taking a shortcut here could affect the final outcome of the mount.

After I retrieve the skin from the degreaser I allow the feathers to dry somewhat. Most degreasers readily evaporate. When the skin has drained and dried for ten or fifteen minutes, invert it and use a towel to pat the surface dry. Then spread a small portion of dry preservative over the entire skin (skip this step if you plan to use a bird tan).

Next, put the skin into a tumbler. If you don't have a tumbler available, you can put a small amount of corn cob grit or another tumbling medium into a thick-walled trash bag with the skin and then slowly shake the trash bag for at least ten minutes or so. Your goal is to fluff the feathers and down, making the skin easier to work with.

The skin will still be damp when it comes out of the tumbler, but the feathers should be full and clean. Use a hair dryer to finish fluffing and drying the down and feathers. This also helps remove any grit or other material that may have gotten into the feathers during the tumbling process. I prefer a hair dryer that has a heat switch. Initially, the heat can be left on to quickly finish the drying process, but as the feathers dry and gain loft it is usually best to eliminate the heat to avoid damage to the skin. I first direct the air onto the neck and head feathers. These are so fragile that I like to get the inside of the skin and the outside feathers dry before continuing with the rest of the bird.

When the fleshing and degreasing process is complete you should have a clean skin with virtually no residue left. This type of skin is a pleasure to work with. Thoroughness with this step will be repaid for years to come because your mount will remain in excellent shape if kept in a good environment.

CHAPTER 6

Preservation Methods

Now that skinning, fleshing, degreasing, and drying are complete, you can turn your attention to preserving the skin. This will allow you to enjoy your work of art for as long as possible, hopefully a lifetime. And with proper care it's possible to achieve this result with your very first mount. Even as your work progresses, and I can assure you that it will if you devote enough time to it, you will enjoy looking back on your first few attempts, not only at the trophy you collected but also at the improvements you made with each new project. Because you want this creation to last, you must choose and properly utilize the best preservation methods available.

If your stay in taxidermy is longer than just one project you will ultimately be sucked into the controversy regarding preservation methods. Debate has raged for many years about the benefits of dry preservative versus a true tan. And as there is no right answer, I'm sure the contest will go on indefinitely.

Advocates of dry preservative note that it is quick and reliable and can achieve a great product. Many world-class taxidermists use nothing but a dry preservative, and they earn blue ribbons and wide respect in national and world competitions. I would guess that around 90 to 95 percent of all bird taxidermy is completed with the use of a dry preservative like Borax. (Borax is the base ingredient of nearly all dry preservatives.)

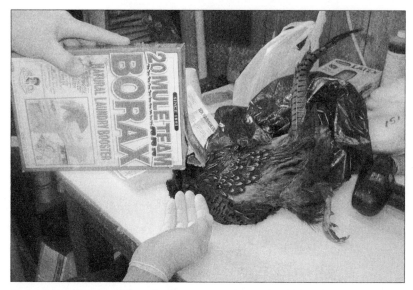

Common Borax is perfect for preserving thin upland bird skins.

There are other taxidermists, however, who swear by only a tanned product, and they compete in national competitions right along with the dry preservative advocates. They may be fewer in number, but they do exist. And as you explore the art of taxidermy further, you will find that the debate over tanning or dry preservative is less lopsided in the field of mammals. Advocates of tanning feel it is a much more effective method of preservation that leads to a longer product life. They also believe it is easier to work with than dry preservative. Complete tanning involves a full list of steps from salting through the final tanning soak, although some modern tanning methods can be done with just a soak in a tanning solution.

You will quickly learn that individual preservation methods vary widely among taxidermists, whether they are hobbyists or full-timers. As you gain experience, you too will form an opinion about the best method.

Let's take a closer look at each method.

DRY PRESERVATIVE

As noted above, dry preservative is the top choice for most professional taxidermists, and for good reason. Most dry preservatives are derived from a powdered chemical substance that if applied properly will preserve and protect the skin from bacteria growth. Most dry preservatives are a mix of chemicals that pull moisture from the skin, discourage bugs from infesting the specimen, and eliminate odors.

Notice I used the word "discourage" bug infestation instead of "eliminate." Borax-based products deter most bugs from penetrating a treated skin, but skins treated with dry preservative can't be considered completely bug proof, so future monitoring and possible treatment with a bug repellant may be necessary.

Dermestids are the number-one enemy of a trophy room. And though the name may not mean a lot to you yet, you will learn more about these bugs as your knowledge of taxidermy increases. Dermestids are actually used in taxidermy to eat flesh. Most methods for cleaning bones and skulls incorporate the use of these tiny beetles, which in abundance can eat the flesh from a large bear skull in less than a week. But these helpful insects can also be a taxidermist's worst nightmare. Most often, by the time damage to a trophy has been found it is too late for anything short of major repair work. And in at least half the cases, the mount is totally hopeless.

Moths can also be detrimental to a mount, probably second only to the dermestid in terms of damage potential. So the knowledgeable taxidermist always keeps a close watch on his trophies.

It's possible to do further bug proofing with dry preservative, but many taxidermists claim it will dissipate with time, leaving the trophy vulnerable to a future infestation. Honestly, I've never had a problem with bugs, nor has any other taxidermist I know. But that's not to say that the situation will not arise in the future. As with any organic product, if conditions become ideal for bugs problems will probably surface at some point. To avoid damage, you must regularly monitor all your mounts and take further steps if necessary.

Though many taxidermists refer to any powdered preservative as a "quick tan," no stabilization of the structural proteins within the skin—the essential element of tanning—actually takes place with dry preservative. So using dry preservative can't be considered tanning.

Dry-preserved skins of any kind, be they mammal or bird, are essentially rawhide that has had the moisture removed. They can return to a raw state at any time if enough moisture contaminates the skin, but the moisture content in the air would have to be extremely high for a very long time to return a dry-preserved skin to such a state. And this extremely high level of moisture would also have a harmful effect on a tanned skin, although it could never return it to a raw state.

Because skin is made up of approximately 60- to 70-percent moisture, it would easily be destroyed by bacteria if left in a natural condition. Dry preservative contains desiccants that drastically reduce this moisture. Desiccants are chemical drying agents that absorb and help prevent the reoccurrence of moisture in the skin. This is how dry preservative got its name: it preserves through a drying action. And because bacteria, which break down the skin, can't exist in a moisture-free environment, no deterioration takes place. So the desiccant-laden dry preservative effectively preserves the skin by keeping it dry.

A second major ingredient in dry preservative is a surfactant. Surfactants help the preservative to better penetrate the skin, allowing the desiccant to do its job. Scientifically speaking, the surfactant lowers the surface tension of the moisture in the skin. This counters the natural tendency raw skin has to repel foreign substances, aiding absorption of the desiccants.

There are some steps you can take to alleviate any problems associated with the dry preservative method. One is to allow whatever dry preservative you choose plenty of time to penetrate the skin thoroughly. It is sometimes best to heavily apply the preservative the evening before completing a mount. Then just fold up the skin and place it on a towel in a cool or refrigerated area. Let it sit overnight before shaking the excess free and reapplying preservative. If this option won't work for you, just make certain that the skin is sufficiently covered with the preservative and fold it skin-to-skin while you finalize preparations for the manikin, wires, any artificial parts, and so on.

I'm getting a little ahead of things here, but once the mounting process is complete you must keep the trophy in a controlled environment. Ideal conditions are between 60 and 80 degrees with relatively low humidity, and these conditions help while you're working, too. In my work area I continually operate a dehumidifier, which keeps the humidity level near 35 percent. This controlled environment is also recommended for tanned products.

It helps the mount to dry in a timely manner, preventing any problems that may occur in a less desirable atmosphere. Early in my career, I mounted animals and birds in my shop and left them there for drying, which is what most taxidermists do. But during the winter temperatures plummeted to the freezing mark nearly every night because I didn't have a constant heat source. As a result, my mounts took considerable time to dry, sometimes up to several weeks. I eventually realized that the longer drying period just helped promote bacteria growth, so during the winter months I began placing all my mounts in a controlled environment.

A major key to quality results with dry preservative is the removal of all fats, muscle tissue, and membranes. If left attached, fats or tissues can cause excessive shrinkage. This is also a factor in the tanning process, of course, but it seems to have a greater effect when dry preserving. With this in mind, it's a good idea to strategically place pins through the skin to keep the major feather tracts from shifting as the mount dries. Also, daily inspections during the drying process can prevent major problems, because if caught in time the feather tracts can be repositioned. Once drying is complete, repositioning becomes all but impossible.

TANNING

Advocates of tanning insist that a tanned skin is much more durable and easier to work with during the positioning stages. This toughened skin more readily takes a stitch because the skin is resistant to tearing. Also, less shrinkage occurs than with a dry-preserved skin, and the color quality may hold up better through the years.

Understanding the chemical composition changes that take place within a skin during the tanning process can help a taxidermist decide which method to use. Those who choose the tanning system usually do so because they like the fact that the skin generally becomes more stable and shrinks less. These factors aren't necessarily of utmost importance for bird taxidermists, though.

To understand the reason for the increased stability you must first understand that skin is a mixture of proteins and moisture. Some of the proteins are soluble and some are insoluble. I once read a very accurate description of skin composition in a "breakthrough" taxidermy manual. The author suggested that taxidermists think of a skin as a leafy tree. The trunk and limbs can be considered the structural, or insoluble, proteins. The leaves represent the blood, fats, and other soluble proteins. To stabilize a skin you must first remove these leaves, leaving only the limbs. But you can't stop at this stage or your tree limbs will eventually collapse because nothing is supporting them.

Basically, this means that when dry preservative is used the bulk of the soluble proteins are pulled from the skin, but they aren't replaced with anything. This is why a bit more shrinkage occurs in a dry-preserved skin. But when tanning is completed properly, the leaves, or soluble proteins, are replaced with tannins, which can be thought of as artificial leaves. These tannins act as fillers that attach themselves to the skeletal, or insoluble, structure. They also help lubricate the structure, preventing it from eventually collapsing and becoming glued together. If done correctly, this results in a more stable skin.

The full tanning process, as it's used for a mammal skin, typically encompasses up to three steps, preceded by salting, degreasing, and washing. Very few taxidermists use this lengthy method of conventional tanning for birds. However, it's important for the budding taxidermist to understand exactly what takes place when tanning a bird or any other skin. For one thing, you may progress from mounting birds to working with a variety of mammals, where tanning is more common. And some taxidermists insist on tanning everything from the smallest bird to the largest mammal.

The best way to start with tanning is to find a tan you're comfortable with and then thoroughly read the directions provided for its use. The steps for each tanning product may vary somewhat.

You begin by applying a layer of salt after the skin has been properly fleshed. This extracts the soluble proteins—blood, fats, and a portion of the oils—from the skin. When salting mammals it may take a day or more to remove these unwanted items, but for birds you only need a couple of hours or so. This is because bird skin is very thin and easily saturated.

Once the salt has done its job you continue by dehydrating, then degreasing and washing the skin. First, shake the excess salt from the skin and place it in plain water. Next, you'll need to degrease and wash the skin to remove excess fats and oils from the skin. As these elements were covered thoroughly in the last chapter, I won't go into detail here.

Now place the skin into a pickle bath, which is a mixture of salt and acid. This further dissolves and removes the soluble proteins within the skin. The acid also breaks the natural bonds of the proteins and prepares the skin fibers to bond with the tannins that will be introduced in the tanning bath. For birds it is important to use a mild acid; for mammals the acid should be a bit stronger. Mix the pickle bath and then check the pH. Ideally, it should fall between 4 and 5. Most acid comes with instructions on how to achieve the proper pH level.

Soak the skin in this pickle solution for forty-five minutes to an hour. After this stage the skin is ready to be placed into the tan.

Soaking the bird skin in a tan replaces the soluble proteins already removed with tannins, which are insoluble proteins. This is a critical step, because without the addition of tannins you might as well have skipped all the previous steps. Just like with the pickle solution, several types of bird tan are available. Initially, you'll have to rely on trial and error to find one that you like or you can get help from taxidermists like those employed by Van Dyke's Taxidermy Supply. Leave the skin in the solution for about an hour. When the feathers are dry you can move on to the next stage in the mounting process.

Remember that the directions for individual products may vary slightly. Some products allow the user to skip several steps. For instance, Knobloch's, a leading manufacturer of tanning products, produces Liqua-Cure, one of the few tans on the market that is bird-specific. With this tan, you simply place a fully degreased soft skin into a solution of one part Liqua-Cure to ten parts water. Salting isn't absolutely necessary with this product; nor is a pickling solution. According to the company, the entire tanning process takes place in one easy step. Just allow the bird skin to remain in the solution for a couple of hours, then remove and mount as usual.

Other companies produce a bird tan that requires only a soak in the tan.

WHICH METHOD SHOULD YOU USE?

The above information should have given you a solid basis for choosing your own method of preservation. Most bird taxidermists still use a dry preservative, but as technology has improved some are opting to thoroughly tan their birds.

Don't let the choice overwhelm you. After many years in the taxidermy business I have formed the opinion that nothing is *always* right or wrong. Advancements in taxidermy usually come from individuals willing to step out and venture where no one else will go, trying new things that no one else will try. I base a lot of my preferences on current circumstances. Some customers just want things done a certain way, or you may have to adjust your methods to deal with a bird that hasn't been cared for well. No matter how you preserve your skins, do the job well and you will reach your goal.

Throughout the rest of the book I will refer to the dry preservative method because dry preservative is very easy to apply and I feel it is 100 percent effective. It's certainly the easiest way for beginners to preserve their bird skins. As your skills improve, you can experiment with various tans for birds and other taxidermy projects.

CHAPTER 7

Premount Preparation

A finished mount is only as good as the field care, skinning, fleshing, and so on. So if you have done a thorough job with each task up to this point, the actual mounting steps ahead should be the easy part. In this chapter I want to focus on the overall mounting process. In the chapters ahead I will progress from detailed looks at easier mounts to more difficult ones.

As you gain experience you will probably want to get more creative with poses, but there is no need to complicate things early on. Certain species and poses require more knowledge, experience, and research than others, and while nothing is written in stone, there are some guidelines worth following for your first few upland birds.

In general, large, tough birds like pheasants or chukar present fewer problems than small birds such as quail. And I recommend starting with a fairly common species. Species that may be difficult to obtain—sage grouse, prairie chicken, mountain quail, certain color phases of ruffed grouse—aren't good choices for your first project because quality reference is usually more difficult to find and they can be a pain to replace if you make a serious mistake. Also, the skin of some birds is much more tender than others. For example, a quail or woodcock would be difficult for a beginner to mount smoothly.

The ideal upland gamebird to start with is a pheasant. Excellent reference photos are readily available, and this bird is

A flying pheasant makes an ideal first mount.

bigger and easier to work with than most other upland species. Pheasants are also easy to obtain, as they are probably the most popular upland gamebird for hunters nationwide. Many game farms around the country raise them for hunting preserves, and adults of both sexes are usually available at a relatively low cost. These pen-raised birds are typically of better quality for taxidermy purposes than wild birds, which may not look too sharp after taking a load of pellets and getting mouthed by an eager bird dog.

Once you have the right bird for your skill level, select a pose that makes life easier for you. A poor choice for the novice taxidermist would be something like a mount with open wings on a pedestal. This is a complicated mount that requires experience and skill to do well. A flying mount attached to a piece of driftwood and placed with the insides of its wings facing the wall would be a much better choice for the beginner. With this mount it is much easier to hide flaws on the underside of the bird, such as the seam areas on the breast and wing incisions.

Except for choosing the perfect bird and pose for your skill level, the preparation of nearly every upland gamebird is identical. You will skin, preserve, wire, and wrap leg and wing bones to replace the muscle tissue that was removed in basically the same way for each new project. Then you will continue with the techniques that are unique for each pose. The differences include what size wire goes into the wings or legs (an open-winged mount requires larger wing wires, while a standing mount requires larger leg wires; and a pheasant would require larger wire throughout than a quail), the particular bodies that will be used, and the final positioning of the mount.

Before continuing, it is best to make sure that your work area is very clean. Lots of effort has gone into maintaining the cleanliness of the feathers so far, and it is just as important to strive for this same goal throughout the rest of the mounting process. If possible, cover your work table with freezer paper or permanently attach a piece of wallpaper or other slick surface. Your main objective should be to create a snag-free surface (to avoid possible feather damage) that doesn't readily hold dirt or debris. After each step, be sure to wipe the surface clean or replace the covering if it is soiled.

Another vital element is starting with a dry bird. Dry feathers add loft and are much easier to work with and position. Immediately prior to the mounting process, I like to use a hair dryer to fluff the feathers one more time. It's not just the feathers that need to be completely dry; the down that lies underneath must also be in perfect condition. This is actually what gives the feathers that full look when they lie against the body. If the down isn't totally dry, the feathers tend to look flat and lifeless.

Once the mount is complete, you should again use a hair dryer to add body to the feathers before final positioning. Some of the feathers may have gotten damp from moisture in the skin slowly seeping out, or they may have been mashed flat from excessive handling.

STEP-BY-STEP

With your work area clean and all the necessary tools at hand, you are ready to start. Place the bird on its back with the underside of the wings exposed. Because you only skinned the wings to the humerus-radius-ulna joint, you must now remove the tissue in the last section of the wing. The reason you don't remove these muscles during the initial skinning process is that water could enter the quills of the wing feathers while you're washing the skin, possibly causing problems. This moisture could eventually sour, causing a bad odor and maybe even mold.

You have two options for removing this tissue. Cut the skin parallel to the radius and ulna on the underside of the wing, which is recommended for beginners, or completely invert the wing and remove the tissue from the exposed bones, which is generally completed during the initial skinning process. (I know this sounds contradictory, but the moisture problem is less likely to occur when totally inverting the wing, without the incision that is most common for commercial taxidermy.)

There are advantages and disadvantages to both options, but if you cut along the underside of the wing the primary feathers remain attached to the ulna, which in turn helps them hold a position very close to that on a live bird. This is the incision you should probably go with until you gain some experience positioning wing feathers.

With the second option, instead of stopping at the humerus-radius-ulna joint during the skinning process you continue to skin past this joint to the opposite end of the radius-ulna joint with the carpals. Be careful skinning down the trailing edge of

Here is the fleshed and inverted wing.

the ulna, as the primary and secondary wing feathers are anchored there and you need to sever them very close to their base. Many competition taxidermists prefer this method because it leaves no seam on the underside of the wing. Thus, the taxidermist is able to mount an open wing that shows no seams or cuts.

This incision is preferable when a bird is to be mounted on a pedestal with open wings, but it is probably best reserved for taxidermists with some experience. If you do it properly you can clean the muscle tissue from the bones slightly better and achieve a slicker appearance, but if not, you will likely have a mess on your hands. Remember, for the best results just start simple and then progress slowly as you gain skills and experience.

To use the first method for removing this additional muscle tissue, cut lengthwise along the radius-ulna bones with a scalpel. This cut should be made from the humerus-radius-ulna joint to the carpals. After the cut is made I immediately place a small amount of dry preservative on the incision. This prevents any fluid from leaking onto the feathers. Now begin working your fingers underneath the skin. Separate the skin on the trailing side of the wing until you can see the feather quills. Then turn your attention to the leading side, gently working your fingers to the front edge of the wing. It is very helpful to reapply dry preservative on these muscle groups from time to time. This allows you to get a better grip on the slippery tissue you're pulling out.

Use the scalpel to begin cutting the muscle tissue free from the trailing side of the wing. Carefully cut until this tissue is loose. Then cut each end and any remaining points that haven't already been severed. Once the trailing side is finished, turn your attention to the leading side again. I like to start cutting this tissue free at the bone and work my way forward.

Cut straight down to the radius bone and then begin cutting the tissue free, working toward the leading edge. You may have to use your fingers more to work the tissue free here. As it loosens, once again sever each end and pull it free. Continue by removing the section of tissue between the radius and ulna. This tissue may be the toughest to remove, especially in smaller birds like quail. In small birds you may have to use a modeling tool to help remove this tightly positioned flesh.

On larger birds I begin by making a cut along the bone on each side of this muscle section. Then I turn the scalpel at a slight angle and use what is almost a prying action until I can get hold of this muscle with my hands. Once I have a decent grip, I gently cut with the scalpel until this muscle tissue is free. Then I add more dry preservative to the opening.

Your goal should be to remove 100 percent of the flesh in the radius-ulna area, although initially this may prove difficult. You can actually do more harm than good by being overzealous, so go slowly. Cut free as much tissue as possible without damaging the outer area of the wing, and then apply a generous amount of preservative. It will take a bit longer to dry thoroughly, but in the end it should be okay, especially for your first few attempts. With practice, you will become much more adept at removing this flesh.

Now you should be ready to wire the wings and legs. For most upland birds, I start with the legs. As mentioned in the tool discussion, wire size will be determined by the desired pose and personal preference, which you'll develop through experience.

For a flying mount, the leg wire only holds the legs up. As it doesn't need to support the weight of the entire mount, #14 wire usually works well for most species from pheasant to quail. The wings are extended, so they require greater support; #12 generally works well for this.

With standing birds, the wire gauges are typically reversed. The legs support the weight of the entire mount, so they require

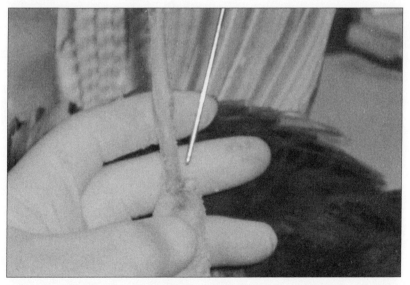

It may be easier to insert the leg wire on the back side of the tibia and then slide it slowly down through the heel of the foot, but on a flying mount there is no reason to run it completely through the foot.

the larger wire. The wings on a standing mount are likely to be closed, so a smaller wire can be used. When choosing leg wire for a standing bird remember that it is best to use a wire that is too large rather than one that's too small. This discourages your bird mount from wanting to lean during the difficult final positioning. Choosing the appropriate wire size for an individual bird will get easier with experience. You should always select wire large enough to firmly support a mount, yet supple enough to shape without undue stress to the skin or feathers.

To begin the leg-wiring process, make a short incision along the heel of the foot. Prepare an appropriate-sized wire by sharpening one end. Now invert the feathered area of the leg skin over the lower featherless area of the leg. Hold the leg in one hand and the wire in the other and insert the wire into the small cut you just made on the heel. The wire should slide easily along the scaled leg and exit at the first joint. If the wire is tough to insert you may want to drop down a size or you may simply need to twist the wire as you're pushing it. (An alternate method is to insert the wire from inside the skin, along the backside of the femur, and down the back of the scaled portion of the leg. This is a good approach for a flying mount because the wire doesn't need to exit at the foot. As a result, no hole is visible at the bottom of the foot.)

Now you are ready to restore the musculature of the leg. Before you continue, though, make sure that enough wire extends past the foot to properly secure the bird to a base later on. On a flying mount the wire doesn't need to extend past the ball of the foot, as it will serve no other purpose beyond positioning the foot.

Begin the rebuilding process with some type of twine. I have found that a dark-colored yarn works great. It is inexpensive and plenty strong enough to complete the task. The dark color helps mask any unnoticed holes in the legs or wings.

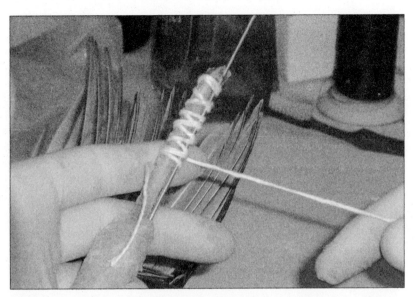

Wrap twine tightly around the wire and leg bone to lock them in place.

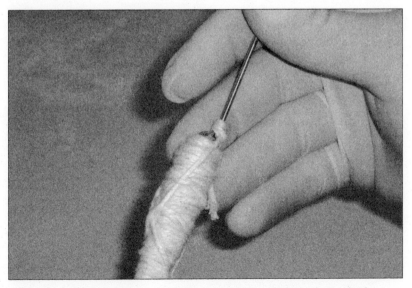

Continue wrapping twine or add filler material to help reshape the leg.

It takes practice to obtain the most accurate shape possible when rebuilding the muscle tissue. But you can help yourself by tracing an outline of the leg onto a sheet of paper or cardboard prior to removing the tissue. For the best results, trace the leg from the side and then the back so you have two angles. Use these outlines as reference to begin forming the leg muscle. On your first attempts it is a good idea to only replace about 70 percent of this muscle tissue, in a general shape. The slack left in the leg makes the skin much easier to position later on.

Squeeze the leg bone and the wire together and begin wrapping from the lower joint of the leg toward the end of the femur. I usually make several passes over the femur to ensure a good coupling. Try to avoid wrapping past the end of the femur onto the wire only, as this makes final adjustment of the wire position more difficult.

Now you have two choices: either wrap the femur and wire with Polyfil or continue with just the yarn. Yarn is usually sufficient for most upland birds, but for larger birds Polyfil takes up much more space with each wrap. Again, it is usually best to rebuild any muscles slightly smaller rather than larger. If you overfill the area, you'll have a heck of a time forcing the skin over the area for positioning. At best, this makes proper positioning difficult; at worst, it could lead to tears.

Now turn your attention to the wings, which can be wired in many different ways. I have found that a wire running the entire length of the wing bones provides more control over the final product. This wire adds stability and makes it easier to position an otherwise limp wing.

First, establish the correct wire size for the type of mount you're attempting. Closed-wing birds don't require as large a wire as those placed in a flying pose. Size 12 is ideal for a flying bird, but on a closed-wing mount the only purpose the wire serves is to anchor the end of the humerus to the shoulder area of the manikin. For some standing mounts a short L-shaped piece of small-gauge wire does the trick. This is simply to keep the wing anchored in a desired area. Initially, this technique may cause problems, though, as the humerus can easily slide off the wire anchor and be a burden to reattach, especially after the breast incision has been closed. Of course, for larger birds these wire sizes should be adjusted accordingly.

To insert the wire along the full length of the wing, slide it through the inside of the skin alongside the humerus, past the radius and ulna, and into the "hand" (carpometacarpus) section. It is okay if the wire protrudes, as long as it can be cut and easily hidden after drying. Again, be very careful when inserting this wire. Hold the wing in one hand and the wire in the other and carefully work the wire in while twisting and pushing until the carpometacarpus is fully penetrated. The goal here is to slide the wire just in front of the hand area while staying within the skin, or just on the underside. For some projects, I

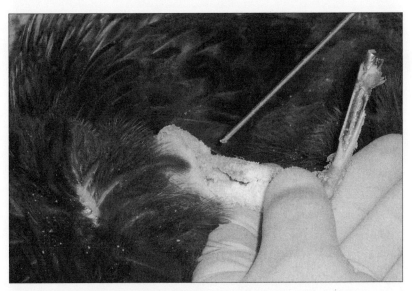

Insert support wire into a fully inverted wing. If the wing can't be fully inverted you will need to slide the wire through the radius-ulna area into the "hand" section. Notice that the humerus (far right) has been repaired with wire.

penetrate the skin and allow the wire to protrude up to ten inches past the exit area. This gives me something to which I can attach tape while stretching over the top of the primary wing feathers, allowing for easier positioning.

After you have attached the wire to the full length of the wing bones, secure it in place by tightly wrapping over the humerus and wire. Begin with several wraps at the humerus-radius-ulna joint. Wrap tightly, and then bend the wire slightly so that it lies just on the forward side of the humerus. Continue wrapping the full length of the humerus. If you don't wrap tightly enough the wire might slide around to the side.

Unless you are creating a competition-level mount, you don't need to rebuild the muscle tissue for pheasants or smaller upland birds. If you choose to rebuild this area exactly, or happen to be working on a much larger bird, here again it pays to trace the shape of the humerus onto paper while the muscle

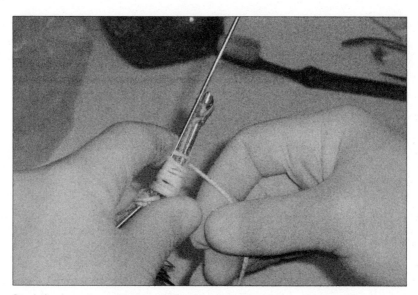

Bind the humerus tightly to the inserted wire. Unless the project is being entered into competition, the muscle tissue in the wing area probably won't need to be rebuilt.

tissue is still intact so that you have some reference for the shape you're trying to duplicate.

With the wing properly wired and wrapped, sew up the openings on the underside. This isn't as important on a closed-wing bird as it is with a flying pose, where the underside of the wings will be visible at times. Now place the wing out of the way and continue with the opposite side. Once both sides are complete the skin is ready for mounting.

In recent years several top taxidermists have marketed artificial heads, necks, and feet. All of these products can help you produce a superior product, and I will elaborate on them a bit more in the upcoming chapters. But at least initially, it will be best to learn the process using the natural feet, the natural head, and a neck cut from neck material.

Admittedly, using an artificial neck is a bit easier, and it may be best to make your first attempts with such presized material, but learning to use raw neck material will increase your knowledge of this procedure must faster. You may want to purchase and study a couple of the artificial necks that you will be using most, as this will also help you to re-create a neck from scratch. It is very valuable to gain a solid understanding of the basics by working with the natural materials. Once these techniques are mastered, you will find it much easier to move on to more advanced methods.

Start with the head. You can actually prep the head before the skin has been wired, but I wait until now so there is less chance of damaging the clay in the head and the eyes while the bird is being handled. Fully invert the skin on the head through the incision made underneath the head and neck. Once the head is fully exposed, coat it thoroughly with dry preservative.

Now fill each eye socket with clay, flush with the sides of the head. Then place the eyes in a natural position. Look closely to make certain they are even in all aspects—height, protrusion, angles, etc. Once you're satisfied, place a very small

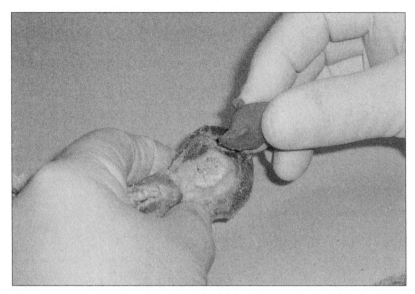

Fill the eye sockets flush with clay. If you add too much the finished head will appear swollen.

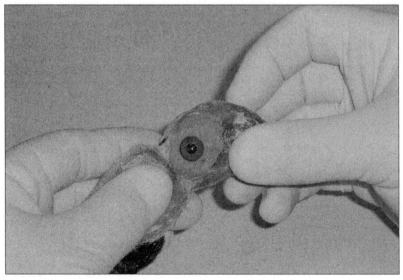

Place each artificial eye into the clay in the center of the eye socket. Make certain the eye positions match perfectly.

ring of clay around each eye; the smaller the better. This ring of clay is used to form a small eyelid and to anchor the eye skin. Reinvert the head and use a sculpting tool and a small soft brush to work with the eye until it is clean and shaped appropriately.

With the bird skin fully wired and the eyes set in the head, the only thing left to do is prep the manikin and attach the neck material. Prepping a bird form is fairly simple. A quality manikin that is well sculpted, with properly placed attachment points, can make life much simpler for the taxidermist. Because you won't be using any adhesive the surface of the manikin doesn't have to be scratched (which is done on some manikins for better adhesion). While you're holding the manikin, notice the small dimpled areas in both the shoulder and knee areas of the manikin. These are the attachment points for the leg and wing wires. At the tail area of the manikin you will see a slot that has been filled in with foam. Remove a small sliver of this

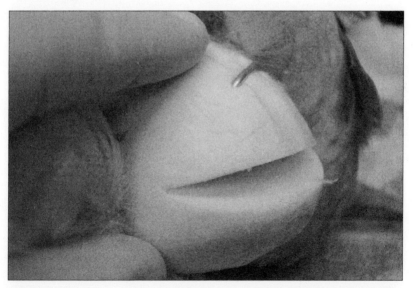

Remove a small sliver of foam from the rear of the manikin to allow room for the tail quills.

foam to allow the tail quills room to slide into place during the mounting process. This makes the final positioning much easier.

Finish the manikin preparation by attaching the neck wire and material. During the skinning process you should have taken a measurement of the neck. If so, use this measurement to cut a piece of flexible neck material. I sometimes find it best, depending on the particular bird and the chosen pose, to cut the neck material slightly shorter than the measurement.

If you didn't get an accurate neck measurement you may have to order a commercially made neck from a taxidermy supplier. These are usually very accurate and easy to work with, unless your bird is of unusual size, which only occurs in rare situations.

To attach the commercial or handmade neck, center the wire in the area where the neck would normally attach. Picture it as an extension of the spine. Now push the wire through

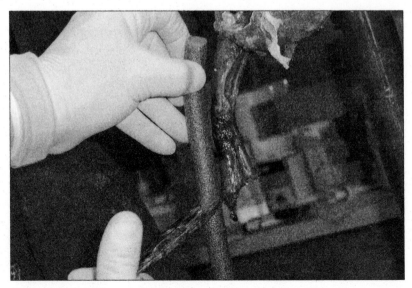

Compare the diameter and length of the artificial neck material to the actual neck to achieve a natural look.

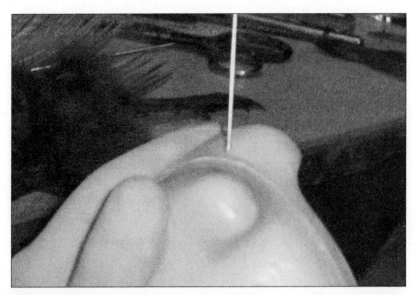

When assembling the neck from neck material alone, you must insert and anchor a neck wire. Study the carcass to locate the proper attachment point.

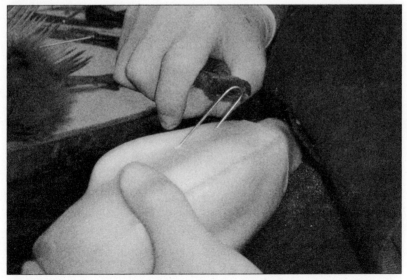

Insert the neck wire completely through the manikin, and then bend the tag end into a "U" shape. Fully seat this excess wire into the manikin.

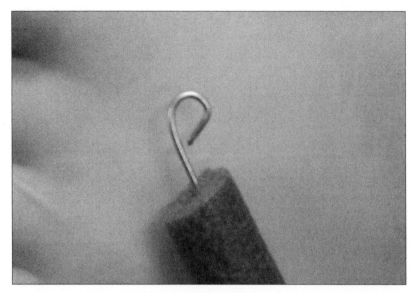

Cut the exposed wire down to slightly more than an inch and bend it to avoid snags while inserting the neck into the skin. If you were able to invert the head without cutting the skin, just leave the wire straight, as there won't be an incision through which to work.

until it exits the manikin in either the back or the breast. Trim the excess wire to within approximately two inches of the manikin. Finish by bending the wire into an "L" shape, and then push the tag end completely back into the manikin. If necessary, use a small hammer to help anchor the wire and to make it flush with the surface of the manikin.

PUTTING IT ALL TOGETHER

We will be using the natural head, so clip any excess wire protruding from the neck material. This procedure is the same for a commercial neck or a wire and natural neck. I usually trim this wire to about one and a half inches past the neck material. It will be used to anchor the head. Initially, it may be easier to insert the wire through the jaw section of the skull, sliding it fully through the nostril opposite the "show" side. Later on, you may choose to trim this wire a bit farther and insert it through the opening in the back of the skull and then anchor it in the forward area of the skull.

Slide the attached neck and wire forward through the neck area toward the head. Go slowly or the wire may snag the skin as it is being inserted. When the neck is nearly in place, insert the extended wire through the skull from the underside, near the back, then work slowly and by feel until the wire protrudes from the nostril that will be displayed closest to the wall. It is usually best to imbed the wire into the forward portion of the skull, possibly into the base of the beak. If you must, drill a larger hole in the rear of the skull and fill it with clay or Apoxie Sculpt, which can be purchased at a taxidermy supplier. Then insert the wire into the rear of the skull and continue.

Be cautious here, because an overly aggressive attempt to pull on the skin or insert wires may rip the skin. With the neck fully inserted, carefully take each wing wire and insert it slowly into the premarked wire placement dimples on the manikin.

Fully insert each wing wire into the premarked location on the manikin.

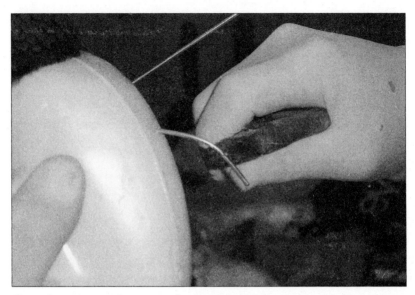

Once the wing is tight against the manikin, bend and reinsert the exit wire to anchor everything.

Slowly work the wire through the manikin until it can be grasped from the opposite side. Once the wire protrudes sufficiently, take the other wing wire and insert it through the opposite side in the same manner. Take your time and fully seat the ends of the humerus wire in the manikin. Then anchor them in place as you did the neck wire.

To finish the premounting process, pull the skin down over the upper breast of the manikin. Don't force it; just pull gently until the skin covers the upper portion of the form. This ensures enough skin length to properly attach the leg wires.

Now attach the leg wires in much the same way you did the wing wires. If you must bend the wire to keep from pulling the skin too tightly, by all means do so. Then the wire protruding from the opposite side of the manikin can be gripped with pliers and slowly pulled until the base of the femur is seated against the manikin. Once you have both legs attached and pulled to the manikin, pull the skin together along the breast

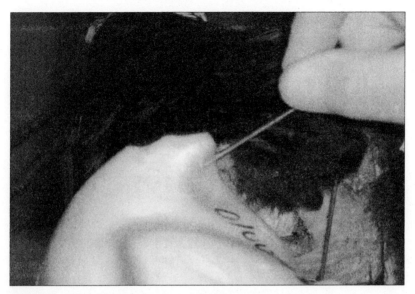

Insert the leg wires into the premarked locations.

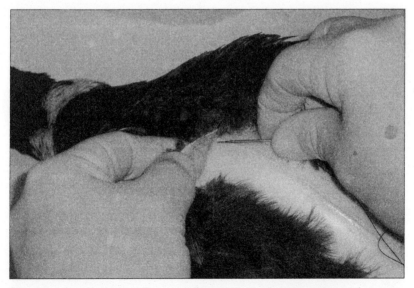

Sew the skin back together, starting near the breast point and moving toward the tail.

incision. Roughly position the wings and legs to allow the skin to come together easily and then sew the incision closed.

Sewing bird skin is very easy as long as you follow a few guidelines. To obtain the best seam, anchor the thread end securely and go slowly at first. Avoid pulling the thread excessively tight because the tender skin may rip. If it does, you'll have to make some repairs and maybe even start over. It's much better to avoid these problems in the first place. Each stitch can be spaced up to a half inch apart as the seam will be well hidden under all the feathers and down material. Just don't snag too many feathers during the sewing process or the mount may have a jagged appearance along the breast.

Tie off the thread tightly when the seam is complete. Then use a regulator or a length of wire to brush the breast feathers forward along the seam. Now gently stroke the feathers back into position with your hand. Finish by plucking any unruly feathers.

You're now ready to continue working on your chosen pose.

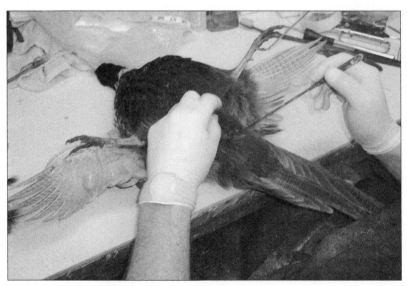

Use a regulator needle to stroke and position the feathers along the seam.

CHAPTER 8

Mounting a Flying Pheasant

L et's start the actual mounting process with a flying pheasant, which is probably the easiest pose and upland bird for the beginner. This may seem odd, but with a standing bird the wings, legs, head, and neck must all be positioned uniformly. And everything must be consistent on both sides of the body. A flying bird allows more room for small variations in posture and balance, so a beginning taxidermist doesn't have to work to such exacting standards.

Picture a human standing motionless. If a model of this supposedly still figure has one leg bent slightly more than the other and one arm raised just slightly to the side and maybe the head craning just a bit forward you will still recognize it as a person, but you will also quickly notice that the appearance isn't natural.

Now picture a person running or dancing. The pose may include flailing, uneven arms and legs, a contorted body, and various head and neck angles—all characteristics of someone in motion. If a model of this moving figure has one leg bent slightly too much, one arm farther from the body than the other, and a head craning forward just a bit these uneven body positions will likely go unnoticed.

The same goes for birds that are being mounted. The uneven wings and awkwardly positioned head of a standing pheasant are much more noticeable than on a flying bird, where these characteristics actually add to the illusion of motion. During the flight of a live bird the feet may be drawn up beneath the bird and the distance between them may vary from moment to moment. The wings may be cupped as the bird comes in for a landing, or they may be high overhead when the bird attempts to gather air for speed or elevation. The head may be angled to the side or high or low when the bird peers to one side or the other or attempts to land. All of this makes a flying pose much more forgiving for the beginner because even if the angles and posture aren't perfectly accurate the mount will remain lifelike.

And a standing mount must be properly balanced over the feet to achieve the correct aesthetic appeal, while a flying mount has no balance point because air from the wings is supposedly holding it aloft. Actually, it would be inaccurate to say that a flying bird has no balance point, but this point changes continuously.

In an earlier chapter I mentioned a few reasons why a pheasant is the best species choice for beginners. This isn't etched in stone, of course, as you can learn taxidermy on many species of upland bird, but pheasants are large and relatively resistant to abuse. Doves and woodcock, on the other hand, are small and fragile and should be avoided until you have a firm grasp on bird taxidermy. The skinning and fleshing procedures are particularly difficult with these birds because their skin is like wet tissue paper. Perhaps the best thing about working with pheasants is the ease of replacement if something goes awry. Many upland species are raised commercially, but species like ruffed grouse are primarily taken by hunting. So if you mangle your first grouse skin and don't happen to have another bird in the freezer, you'll have to wait until the next hunting season.

Now that I have restated my case for starting with a flying pheasant, let's get down to details of the final mounting process. The premounting procedures outlined in the previous chapter are basically the same for most any species and pose, so we can pick up right where we left off.

At this point, the wings and legs should be properly wired, all the muscle tissue replaced with a filler material, and any incisions sewn up. There is nothing left to do but study your reference material and position the pheasant in the appropriate manner and then permanently attach it to a piece of driftwood or a panel. Bases are covered in a later chapter, but it helps to know that flying mounts can be temporarily fixed to any type of wood until a final base is chosen. This isn't true for standing mounts, though, which should be attached to the final base right away so the feet can dry in a shape that fits the base.

There are no set rules for what needs to be attended to first, but I have found it best to get into the habit of starting in one area, getting it roughly positioned before moving to the next one. When you have everything more or less in position, start again in the same order to apply the final touches to each area. Apply tape to any area that needs it and groom any unruly feathers.

If everything up to this point has been done properly, the final phase of mounting should be relatively easy. And it will become even easier with each project. If you find that the final positioning is extraordinarily difficult and the feather patterns and limbs do not align properly, stop right there and assess what may be causing the trouble. The most typical problem is probably a manikin that is too large. If this is the case, don't hesitate to disassemble the mount and try again. Attempting to proceed will only cause further frustrations.

Wing positioning will be determined by whether you choose to mount the bird with a side, front, or back view. For example, most frontal views include sharply cupped wings, as if the bird were coming in for a landing. The side view typically incorporates very high wings, as if the bird were trying to gain elevation or speed. A back view generally simulates a bird that is gliding or turning, with little, if any, aggressive wing positioning. Study your reference material carefully to achieve the right posture.

In this chapter we are mounting a pheasant with a back view. As mentioned previously, this helps hide the area underneath the wings, as well as the ventral incision used for most mounts.

I like to begin the final positioning with the legs. These are easy to deal with on a flying bird because they are usually bent at the joint between the feathers and scaled leg area and the foot simply pulled forward. The width between the feet isn't a major factor, so position them in way that looks natural and move on to the wings. The feet aren't used to support anything on a flying mount, so it isn't necessary to extend the wire past the ball of the foot. If this has already been done in the pre-mounting procedures, just clip the protruding wire flush with the foot and continue.

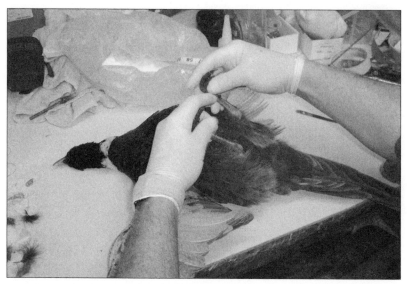

Bend the legs gently until they appear naturally drawn in under the body for flight. It's okay if the angle of the legs varies a bit because birds are constantly making adjustments as they fly.

The wings should already be extended evenly and nearly perpendicular to the body of the mount. Be careful to not overextend the wings, but also avoid extending them too little. Again, use reference photos to help ensure accuracy.

Once the wings and feet are in their approximate positions, spread the tail slightly and make certain it has been inserted into the tail slot. Then position the head using reference photos and your own imagination.

The wings should be close to their final position after the initial wiring. Just make minor changes to get them exactly where you want them.

Spread the tail and hold it in place with tape or cardboard and staples.

While the skin is limp and wet, work through several positions for the head and neck until you are satisfied. Many beginning taxidermists are hesitant about being creative with their work. Creativity and confidence usually come with experience, but it's important to position the head and neck with natural curves. A straight-as-a-stick posture never appears lifelike. I typically mount flying pheasants at an angle if they are going to be attached to the wall. The bird appears to be banking to one side or the other. I bend the neck downward and pull the head away from the wall. This pose simulates a bird that has passed its intended landing point and is circling back.

Once you have the entire bird roughly positioned, it's time to attach support wire and tape, groom any unruly areas, and make any final adjustments.

To wire a flying mount, you must install attachment points on the wall side of the bird. This is best done with 10- to 14-gauge wire, depending on the particular bird. For this project,

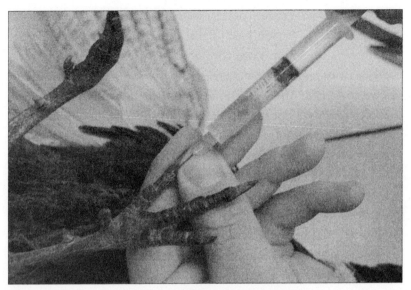

If you haven't already done so, inject liquid preservative into the feet and fleshy areas of the wings after the initial adjustments.

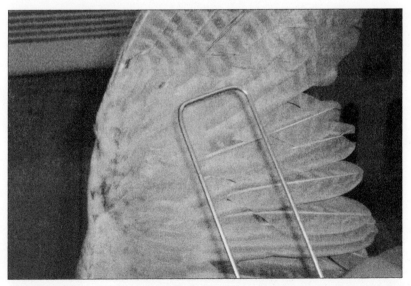

Notice the shape of the wire that will be pushed flush underneath the wing to hold it up.

12-gauge should suffice. Begin with a section of wire that is twenty-four inches long, and sharpen each end to make the insertion process smoother. Now grip the wire about eleven inches from one end with a pair of pliers and bend it at a right angle. Grip the wire again approximately eleven inches from the end of what is now the longer section and make another bend like the first one. You should be left with a wire that resembles an eleven-inch-long staple.

Be very careful attaching the wire. If some damage occurs it can probably be fixed because the skin remains maneuverable, but it's still a hassle that is better avoided. Hold the body of the mount and slightly lift the wing that will be positioned closest to the ground (or farthest from the wall). Begin inserting the wire at the base of the wing and angle it slightly so the exit point is on the opposite side of the breast point. Once both sharpened ends exit the manikin, grip the protruding wires with pliers and pull them until the wire on the other side has seated firmly and completely. Now the two sharpened ends on

Insert the doubled wire through the mount so it exits near the point of the breast.

the back side of the breast can be bent for attachment to a piece of driftwood or a panel or just something temporary.

The final wiring step starts with two 14-gauge wires sharpened on one end. Insert a wire an inch or more into the manikin underneath each wing. The exact position is usually along the trailing edge of the primary and secondary wing feathers. Bend the wire slightly to form a natural curve that conforms to the flow of the wing. After both wings are finished, use masking tape to lightly secure them in their final positions. Make certain that each feather slightly overlaps the last in a natural way and groom each wing until it resembles your reference photos.

With the wiring complete, give the mount a gentle overall grooming to smooth out or eliminate unruly feathers. A few feathers may have to be plucked, while others may be tamed with tape.

You must also position the eyes properly and shape them according to appropriate reference. Take your time with this

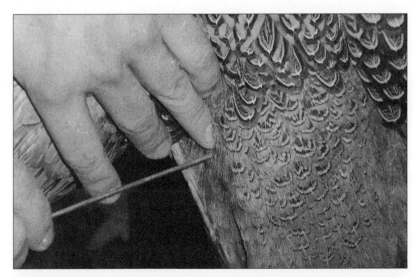

To help support the trailing edge of each wing, insert a sharpened wire under each wing and then bend the wire gently until you achieve the desired position.

Attach tape to the support wire, which exits near the wingtip, to spread the wing outward and hold it in place.

It's a good idea to tape the beak closed before completing the final positioning of the head and eyes.

procedure, as it can be one of the most difficult aspects of mounting an upland bird. It's also one of the most visible, so doing it correctly will go a long way in making your final mount look professional.

Final shaping and positioning of the eyes is most easily learned through experience, but I'll do my best to point you in the right direction. Always rely more on reference material than the instructions, or opinions, of others. To obtain the most life-like appearance, start by positioning the eyes at the same depth and angle. I actually think it's preferable to have both eyes incorrectly positioned but matching than to have one eye correct and the other incorrect.

When you have them positioned where you want them, form a round opening with the surrounding eyelid—leaving a small corner in the front of the eye—based on your study of reference photos. Now place a very small portion of the eyelid onto the eye along the entire circumference. Dampen a small, soft paintbrush and clean the eye and the surrounding tissue, gradually making minor adjustments as you go. Stop for a moment after you finish and again compare your work to the reference material you have.

The skin of the lower eyelid actually folds into itself to form the eyelid of the pheasant. The eyelids on most birds close upward, rather than downward as in mammals.

If the mount doesn't measure up, start over. With practice, positioning the eyes will become easy for you.

Finally, I like to leave my work for a few hours to get my mind off it before returning to touch it up. Sometimes this is all it takes to get a new perspective on the subject. This is also a good idea if you're encountering frustrating problems. A breath of fresh air and a break can make all the difference.

One final note: On pheasants, it is important to take a light grip on the wattles and pull them gently to achieve a full, fleshy look. After positioning each side, cut a piece of thin cardboard or thick construction paper to match the wattle areas. Place a cutout next to each one, and then use a paper clip to secure it to the lower portion of the wattle, which should be hanging a bit lower than the head. This will discourage the wattle from shrinking as it dries.

When you're satisfied that everything on the mount is correct, place it out of the way for at least a week so it can dry properly. Once it is dry, you can simply remove the paper and paper clip on the wattles and finish normally.

Once the mount has been positioned and taped, take a break so you can return to the work table later with a fresh perspective.

CHAPTER 9

Mounting a Standing Grouse

U pland birds are all beautiful creatures, but the ruffed grouse is certainly one of my favorites. It doesn't have the gaudy colors of a pheasant, but its quiet beauty has captivated many generations of hunters. It is most closely associated with bird hunting in the Northeast and upper Midwest, but it is also found in mountainous country throughout Canada, much of the Northwest, and down through the southern Appalachians. It is an exciting bird to hunt, and its quick, nerve-shattering flushes from thick cover make it a particularly challenging target. On the downside, the ruffed grouse is one of the few birds you won't find at game preserves, which makes it difficult to get a completely undamaged specimen for mounting.

Other species of grouse include the blue grouse, spruce grouse, sharp-tailed grouse, and sage grouse. The first two are found primarily in mountainous areas out west and/or across much of Canada, while the latter two are more closely associated with the western prairies. In either case, geographical limitations make them all less accessible to hunters nationwide than the ruffed grouse.

The distinctive dark tailband is the most dominant feature on the ruffed grouse, which is a mottled brownish color overall. A black "ruff" of feathers around the neck and upper back is more prominent on males, although it's not a foolproof way to identify the sex of a bird. (Males have two white dots on the individual rump feathers, versus one on females, and an unbroken tailband.) Because of its size, the ruffed grouse is a treat to work with.

The colors of a grouse can be displayed equally well on a flying or standing mount. The medium-length tail feathers and black ruff in the neck and shoulder area combine to offer a beautiful mount in either pose.

As discussed in the previous chapter, mounting a standing bird can be a bit more difficult than a flying bird because the balance points and anatomy must be much more accurate for a lifelike appearance.

The premouting steps for a flying or standing bird are basically the same, although the wiring within the wings isn't absolutely necessary because the wings will later be folded and inserted into the wing pockets. The method many taxidermists use for standing mounts is to bend a short piece of small-gauge wire into an "L" shape and then insert one end into the hollow

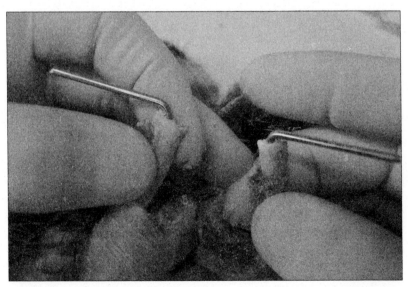

Here two wires have been bent into an "L" and inserted into the ends of the wing bones.

end of the humerus, or uppermost wing bone. Next, insert the free end of the wire into the premarked spot for the wings on the manikin to help hold the wing bones in position. The only problem with this technique is that the wire may pull free from the humerus while you're attaching the legs or sewing up the incision. It's no big deal if it does, though; just carefully work it back into position.

Once all the seams are closed, begin final positioning by attaching the unfinished mount temporarily to a square piece of plywood or the final base. With a standing mount, it is often easier to attach the feet to the permanent base right away. Not only will this save you time later on, but it will also allow the feet to dry in their final position. (If they dry flat on a piece of plywood, they won't look natural when transferred to a curved base.)

Driftwood or small dioramas with rocks, dirt, and other natural objects are the most popular permanent bases, but for this project I'll be using a whitetail antler. Whitetails are found

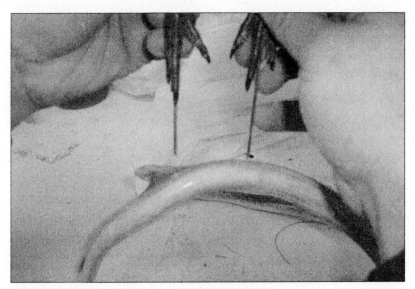

The base for this project is a shed whitetail antler.

throughout most of the grouse's home range, and the antler is just an attractive enhancement for the mount.

Regardless of the material you choose for a base, you must drill holes into it so you can secure the wires extending from the balls of the feet. Mark the correct positions for drilling by holding the legs with the wire extending straight toward the base. Then space them at a natural width, after first studying reference photos. Once you have the feet where you want them, use the wire ends to scratch light marks in the wood for hole positions. Drill 3/32- to 1/8-inch holes, which should easily accommodate the largest wire used for upland birds.

Now insert the leg wires and pull them through until the feet are firmly pressed against the base. Bend the tag ends at right angles, which helps hold the wires in place. Complete the attachment by inserting 3/4- to 1-inch wood or Sheetrock screws up through the wire holes. When the screws are tightened,

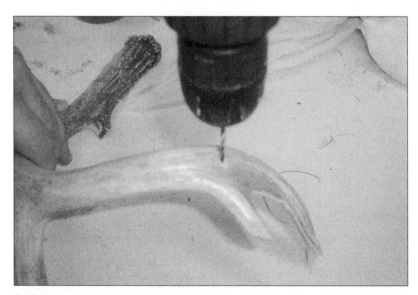

Drill two small holes through the base to accommodate the leg wires. Be careful not to make these too large if using an antler, as you won't be using screws to anchor the wire from below.

they will lock the wires in place against the base. If this is your final base, grip the excess wire ends and bend them back and forth until they break free. If you are using a temporary base for some reason, leave the excess wire intact. You'll need it again when you place the mount on its permanent base.

When the mount attached to the base, look it over and attempt to balance it naturally and evenly over the feet. This can be difficult if you're just starting out, but like everything else, it becomes much easier with experience. Just get the mount roughly positioned for now. As the body posture begins to take shape, you can continue to make adjustments until the mount is nearly perfect. I use the word "nearly" because there is always room for improvement, no matter how long you've been doing taxidermy. It's a never-ending quest for perfection.

Check the angle of the body over the feet. The legs of most upland birds start almost two-thirds of the way back from the

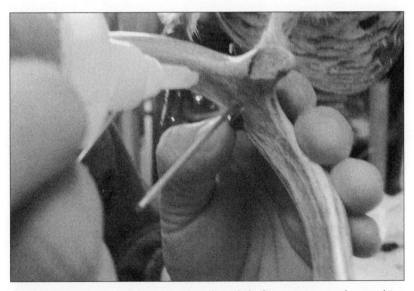

Cut the leg wires to the appropriate length before permanently attaching the feet. The wires are anchored with an instant adhesive and the toes wrapped around the antler and secured.

front of the body. This means that the grouse's body would look unnatural if mounted parallel to the ground. If a live bird tried to stand like this it would immediately topple over. Instead, the body must be tilted slightly at the front to put some of the weight further back toward the rear of the bird, making it appear more balanced. There is no substitute for carefully studying reference photos or live birds to achieve the best balance point. Look for birds that are walking, standing on two feet, or standing on one foot. Pay close attention to the body angle with each stance and you will quickly learn a great deal about balance.

Once you achieve a rough balance point for the legs, continue with other parts of the body. I usually move on to the neck and head. Our standing grouse will be mounted in an alert position, looking slightly to the right. To match this pose, return to your reference photos. You will eventually notice the slight curvature of the neck as it exits the body and again as it turns to the head. If you're using an artificial neck, which I highly recommend for beginners, you will have a neck for a standing bird that is, for the most part, already accurately positioned. If not, carefully bend the curves into the material.

Next, position the head. I prefer not to position the head straight on because this makes the mount appear too rigid. Swivel the head slightly, or even strongly, to one side or the other. Think about where the mount will be displayed after completion and what mood you're trying to create when you're determining the proper head angle. Step back and make certain the head is almost perfectly vertical and that you have an even and consistent flow along the entire length of the neck and into the head.

When you are satisfied that the head and neck look natural, place the tail quills into the precut slot. These quills should slide easily into place. Form a "T" with a short section of 12- to 14-gauge wire and insert the bottom end just under the quills, sliding it into the manikin until the top of the "T" is about a third of the way between the base of the tail feathers and the manikin. This helps support the tail feathers, but allows you to further adjust the angle of the tail. It should flow with the back of the bird, but depending on the mood of the bird the tail may be spread widely (a strutting bird) or fully closed (a walking bird).

Spread the tail feathers slightly, making certain that each feather correctly overlaps the previous one. This usually starts with the center, and longest, feather on top. The slightly shorter adjacent feathers should be placed just underneath the center one, continuing out to the last, and shortest, feather on each side. Most upland gamebirds fly with their tail feathers spread, but close them when sitting calmly. One option with a standing mount is to spread the tail slightly, just for aesthetic appeal. Many birds do this while preening; just be careful not to overdo it. Tweak it as needed, and then move on to the wings and feather tracts.

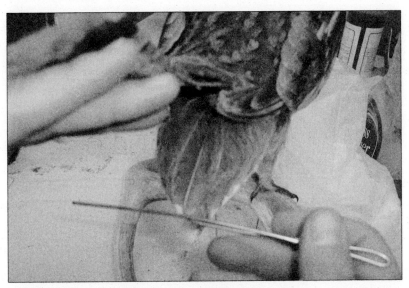

Raise the primary tail feathers and insert the "T" support wire just above the feathers underneath.

Spread the tail and secure it with tape.

If the right-sized manikin was used and the wings and legs were attached in the appropriate places, the wings should slide easily into place. Locate the wing pockets, which should be easy to find on virtually any bird. They are on each side of the breast and generally fall slightly away from the body after mounting is complete and the wings are pulled away from each side. Now pull the wing pockets outward, pull the wing rearward by the tip, and then fold and slide what would be considered the wrist on a human into the forward area of the wing pocket. If you can't do this without undue force, just carefully work the wing into its proper position and make a mental note to be more conscious of measurements and limb attachment on the next project.

The wing positions for closed-wing mounts will vary slightly among different species of upland bird, but typically the wingtips will be very close to one another, almost touching. In some species, the ends of the wingtips actually cross slightly.

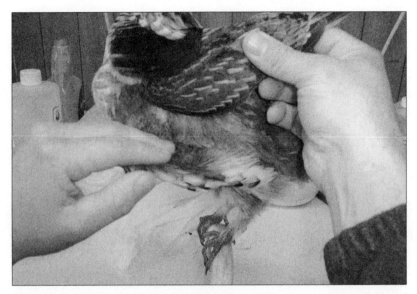

The wings should slide easily into place. Pull gently rearward, then fold and push them forward into the wing pocket.

Study reference photos to get this aspect just right, and do your best to make the wings mirror images of one another. The wings should balance evenly in the wing pockets, and the tips should be even in length as they lie over the back and near the tail. View the mount from each side, from above, and from the front and rear. If necessary, use a ruler to measure the distance from the base to the bottom of each wing, then make adjustments. In most cases, you can just do this step by eye.

When you're satisfied with the wings, start working on the feather tracts. One important area is the wing pockets, which are simply an extension of the sides of the breast feathers. Make sure the feathers flow evenly, without any disruption. The feather tract along the back is also vital for a lifelike appearance, as these colorful feathers have light-colored centers that will catch the eye if out of place.

The last major feather tract is the scapulars, or shoulder feathers. These are sometimes overlooked due to their dark

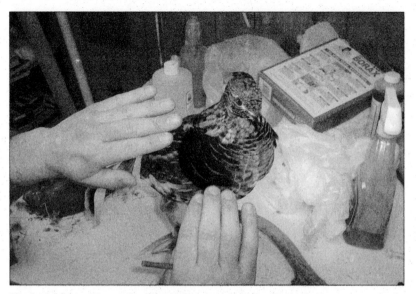

Black feathers along the shoulders are a prominent feature on a male ruffed grouse. Spread these lightly for a lifelike appearance.

coloration, but proper positioning is still necessary for a natural appearance. The scapulars are easily distinguishable from the back feathers because they are in a group at the base of the wings, and they are usually slightly longer than other feathers on the body.

With all features of the standing mount in their approximate positions, start over again to ensure that the mount is even and balanced, that all limbs are in a natural position, and that all feather tracts and individual feathers are groomed and natural. Use masking tape to hold the primaries and secondaries of the wing in the proper position, along with the primaries of the tail and any unruly feathers you notice. You may even have to tape the beak shut to keep it closed.

CHAPTER 10

Mounting a Flying Quail

Mounting one species of upland bird is pretty much like mounting all the rest. Some species are more delicate than others, some more colorful, and some have fleshy areas (such as wattles) and some don't, but the same basic techniques apply for everything from the small bobwhite quail to the huge sage grouse. The differences between mounting a quail and a pheasant are much like the differences between working on a deer and an elk. Both are in the deer family, but one takes considerably more work than the other.

To reach this stage of mounting a flying bobwhite quail, you must take great pains to avoid tearing the skin or pulling too many feathers loose. Dove and woodcock are probably the only species more delicate than the bobwhite. If your first project was a flying pheasant, you should now be well prepared for the level of care necessary with quail. From a more practical standpoint, the only difference is the size of the wire used.

If you're doing a conventional breast-to-the-wall flying pose 16-gauge wire is all you need to attach the bird to the base. Fourteen-gauge wire works for the internal structure in the open wings. The legs on a flying mount don't support any weight, so you can get by with 16- to 18-gauge leg wire. If you ever mount a standing bobwhite, increase those wires to 14 or 16 gauge.

Bobwhite quail are beautiful trophies, especially when mounted in a group. What the diminutive bobwhite lacks in

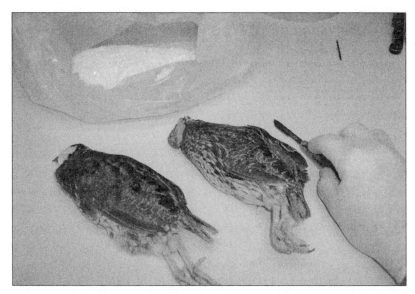

Male (left) and female bobwhite quail are small but beautiful. They make nice trophies, although you must take extra care when working with their delicate skin.

color, it more than makes up for in character. And the long tradition of hunting this species in the South only adds to the appeal. Pen-raised quail are common in most areas, so replacing a damaged bird is relatively easy.

I won't go back through the entire skinning process for quail, but some of the areas you should pay particular attention to when skinning are shown in the accompanying photographs. (For general procedures related to mounting a flying bird, refer back to chapter 8, Mounting a Flying Pheasant.) As always, use reference photos to create the most lifelike mount possible.

Quail are so small that it is relatively easy to make adjustments during the final positioning. On the other hand, anchoring such a small bird can be a real chore because it is tough to push two wires through the manikin without damaging the feathers or skin. To mitigate this damage, increase the wire gauge by one size, in this case to #14. Next, sharpen and insert

Cut along the ridge of the breast, and then sprinkle dry preservative in the incision to soak up any moisture.

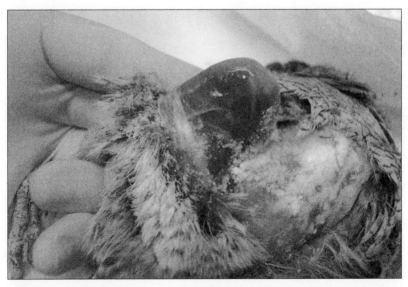

It is easy to tear the skin when severing the leg joint, so work slowly and carefully.

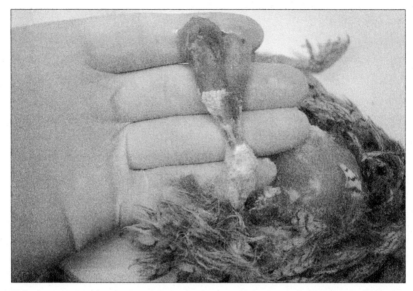

Take extra care with the skin being inverted around the humerus and the leg bone.

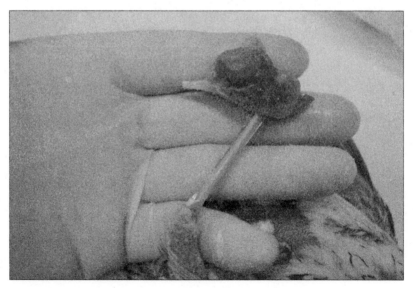

Remove the muscle tissue just as you would with any bird.

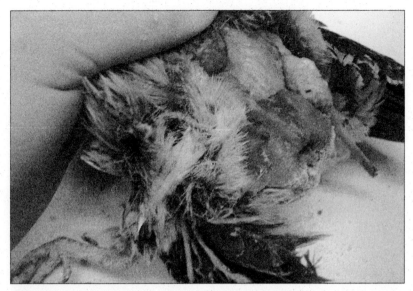

Because a quail's bones are smaller and the skin thinner than on most up-land birds, you must be very gentle when severing the tail and detaching skin along the back.

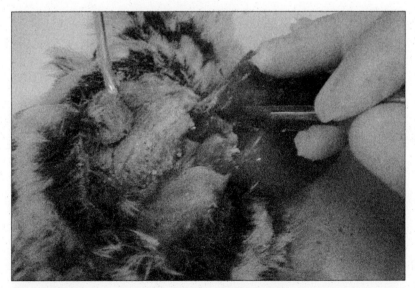

The wing/body junction isn't buried as deeply within muscle tissue as it is on larger birds.

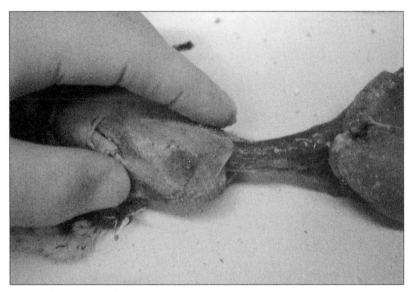

The head usually inverts easily, but don't force it. If it won't fully invert for some reason, just sever it and proceed accordingly.

Here is a fully inverted head. Keep in mind that the head skin and eyelids are extremely fragile.

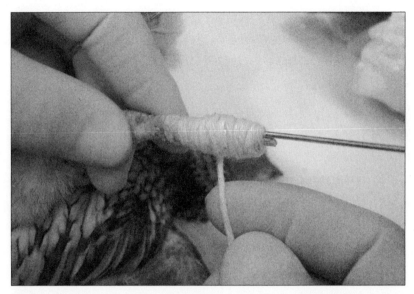

Replace muscle tissue the same way you would on other birds, but on a smaller scale.

After the wings, legs, and head are attached, it's time to sew up the breast incision.

only one end under the wing that will be tilted toward the ground, or farthest from the wall after hanging, at an angle that allows it to exit near the point of the breast. With the wire inserted almost completely under the wing, bend the last four inches into a right angle on the insertion side. Then bend the final two inches of wire so it is parallel to the main wire, like a small hook. Pull the wire through the exit hole until the bent portion at the insertion point under the wing is fully imbedded in the manikin.

This anchoring technique is nearly identical to the method previously discussed, except that now there is only one hole in the skin on each side of the bird. Another advantage is that final positioning should be easier after the mount is attached to the wall, as only one wire must be adjusted versus two with the standard method.

Once the supporting wire is attached securely to the mount, drill a small hole through a panel or driftwood base and insert the wire until the mount is at the desired distance. With small birds like quail, I prefer to place several mounts on a piece of medium-sized driftwood. If you mount a single small bird on a large piece of driftwood the base may seem out of proportion and may draw attention away from the mount. When you only have one quail-sized bird to mount, just make sure the base is relatively small so the material enhances rather than overpowers the bird.

Final positioning is ultimately up to the individual taxidermist, but I prefer a flying mount to be angled slightly upward, with the head pulled slightly away from the wall.

To get an approximate final position, adjust the bird so its body is slightly less than 45 degree beyond horizontal. (Perfectly horizontal positioning would be parallel to the floor.) With a pheasant, you usually have to make allowances for the upper wingtip as you adjust the angle of the bird to the wall, but quail are so small that this isn't a concern. Simply adjust the bird to a position that appeals to you.

Next, bend the wire extending through the back of the base to hold it in place, and then secure it permanently by tightening a screw into the hole (again from the back of the base and into the same hole as the supporting wire). This should lock the wire in place, but if you have any doubts just drill a smaller hole adjacent to the first one so that it is barely large enough to accommodate the wire. Then insert the tag end of the wire into this new hole and tighten an appropriate-sized screw in place.

Carefully check the look of the quail, starting with one specific area and moving on to each successive area. Repeat the process to be completely sure you've positioned every aspect for maximum aesthetic appeal. Due to the bird's small size, you can usually finish this detailing quickly. Let's run through the steps, starting with the head and neck.

The neck is short, so it can just be pulled slightly downward. But you must be more cautious with the head position. The action, or flow, you put into the mount is clearly visible in the neck and head positioning. Put the head straight above the neck and the mount will look stiff and unnatural. A better idea is to shape the head and neck so the bird appears to be actively searching for a place to land, a predator to avoid, or perhaps a food plot. I like to pull the head slightly away from the wall and bend it down gently toward horizontal. These adjustments will be minor on a bird this size.

Next, adjust the wings so they appear to be working together. They should be extended in a natural position appropriate for the attitude of the mount. In other words, they should not appear to be overspread or underspread. When you have them where you want them, insert a piece of light-gauge wire underneath each wing.

These support wires—one on each side—should be placed along the trailing edge of the primary and secondary feathers. Patiently shape the wire until you achieve a natural flow from the body out toward the wingtip, and secure the wingtip of each wing to the corresponding support wire with masking tape. Then carefully separate each feather to enhance the gentle flow down the wing and apply masking tape along the show side of the wing feathers. This locks them in position while the mount dries. Be sure to anchor the secondary feather closest to the body tightly against the body to ensure a smooth appearance and to hide any loose feathers or down underneath the wings.

Now move on to the tail. Bend a short piece of 18-gauge wire in the shape of a "T"; this wire will be inserted under the tail for support. After shaping, this wire should be no longer than three inches. Lift the tail slightly and push the wire in until it's firmly seated in the manikin, and then spread the tail feathers and allow them to lie on top. Spread the feathers evenly across the entire tail, much the same way you shaped the wing

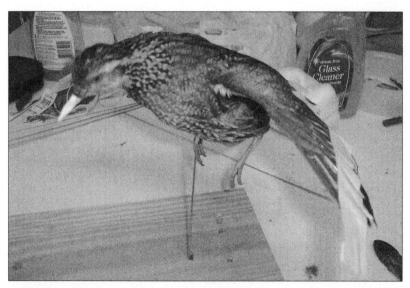

This quail was mounted as part of a flushing covey being attacked by a predator, so the support wiring was placed through the breast to hold the bird horizontal to the ground. It has been positioned and taped and is ready for drying.

feathers. Secure them in place with masking tape. Remember, the desired shape isn't flat and lifeless. The tail should form a shallow arch.

The legs are usually the easiest body parts to position on a flying upland bird mount. Unless the bird is coming in for a landing, the legs may simply be tucked up under the rear of the body. Fold the legs up, if you haven't already done so, and secure them in place with masking tape if need be.

The mount should be almost complete now. Check for any unruly feather areas, tweak the position of each individual area, and go over the entire mount until it matches your reference photos. It would be impossible to overemphasize the importance of reference material. It is your closest link to a natural appearance.

Finally, place the mount out of the way to dry.

CHAPTER 11

Finishing and Base Attachment

UPLAND BIRD FINISHING BASICS

All taxidermy projects require some level of finishing. Some mounts, such as fish, require extensive finishing work—repairing seams and low spots with fillers and blending colors to create a lifelike appearance. I would put mammals somewhere in the middle, as they typically require a little extra work around the eyes, nose, and ears. But I think birds are the easiest projects when it comes to finish work.

How you go about finishing will depend somewhat on whether you used the natural head or an artificial head. With an artificial head, you will need to complete the painting process prior to mounting, but in most situations the natural head will require little, if any, additional color to the beak only. (The beak of an artificial head must be painted.) You may have to make some repairs to a natural head due to shot damage, and in extreme cases it might be easier to go with an artificial. To be honest, though, I never have fully understood the concept of an artificial upland bird head. It just doesn't seem necessary. I recommend that you use the natural head, but you should know that the other option is available.

It is relatively easy to finish nearly every species of upland bird. The most difficult aspect is learning to use an airbrush properly and choosing the appropriate paints and colors. This can only be accomplished through experience and trial and error. Most upland birds have dark-colored legs and beaks, so you won't need to experiment too much. The only major exception is the ring-necked pheasant, which has bright red wattles on the sides of the head.

Start by acquiring an affordable but quality airbrush. Next, choose a high-quality wildlife paint and stick with that brand. Using just one brand while you're learning the ropes will help you get familiar with its nuances. There are several good paints available, and I can't really recommend one brand over another. The only major difference in paints is that they are either lacquer based or water based. Many veteran taxidermists, myself included, typically prefer lacquer-based paints. These dry quickly and can be blended easily, and they generally produce an excellent finish. The disadvantage to lacquer-based paints is that you must use a respirator and work in a well-ventilated area because they are flammable.

This leads some taxidermists to try water-based paints. They aren't flammable, although a respirator is still recommended, and it can be argued that they have a higher luster when dry. The downside is that you must let each layer of paint dry for several minutes before you add the next coat.

For upland bird taxidermy, I think you could choose either type and be happy.

There are no hard and fast rules for finishing upland birds. The best advice I can offer is to become adept at using your airbrush and refer constantly to your reference photos. Always try to avoid getting paint on the small feathers adjacent to the head and feet, and apply colors lightly until you achieve the perfect coloration.

It would be difficult to include a finishing or coloration chart for all upland birds. Thankfully, the feet are the only area that must be finished on most birds. The feet and scaled portions of the legs tend to dry a much darker color than what you see on a live bird, so you'll need to restore the brighter original shade.

Some taxidermists even like to mist a light coat of satin or gloss finish on the beak and feet to give them a shiny appearance. If you go this route, just be careful not to apply too much. In fact, it may be wise to avoid applying any gloss at all until you've progressed past the learning stage.

Let's take a closer look at the pheasant, as it's usually the only major upland bird that requires paint to the head. Pheasants have a large, bright red wattle on each side of the head, and these fade to a brownish color after drying. I use bright red paint and a regular paintbrush to restore the original shade. Dip the brush lightly into the paint, and then dab paint on lightly to avoid getting any on the eyes. Continue slowly until the wattles are completely finished; use reference to determine the exact color.

The bright red wattles on a pheasant require special attention with a paintbrush.

ATTACHING THE BASE

Most bird mounts are simply attached to a piece of driftwood. Whether the mount is standing or flying, driftwood pieces seem to look natural. For a standing bird you should find a piece that fits well. In other words, you need a piece that is relatively flat and big enough to hold the mount erect without the possibility of tipping. Also, as mentioned previously, it is usually best to

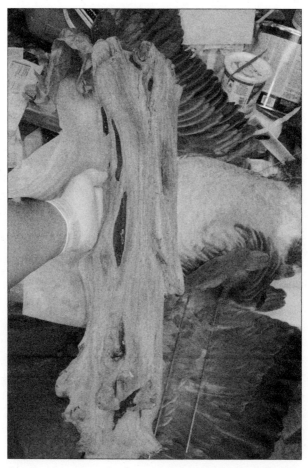

Driftwood is the most popular base material for upland bird mounts. Just be sure the piece you select is sized for the bird being mounted.

attach a standing bird directly to the driftwood before the mount dries. If the feet were to dry in a flat position and you then tried to place them on a rounded base it wouldn't look natural. If you attach the feet to the round base before they dry they will conform perfectly to the surface. Keep this in mind when you're choosing a base for your standing mount.

The best reason to attach a flying mount to the final base before drying is just to avoid the extra work involved in transferring it later on. Because the feet don't need to conform to the base, it really doesn't matter whether or not they are dry when the base is added.

You can search out your own driftwood for the base or purchase a piece from a taxidermy supplier. I recommend the latter option because driftwood from a supplier is usually sized and cut perfectly and has already been cleaned and tumbled. I have also found that, depending on your geographical area, most natural driftwood isn't as dense as the driftwood you

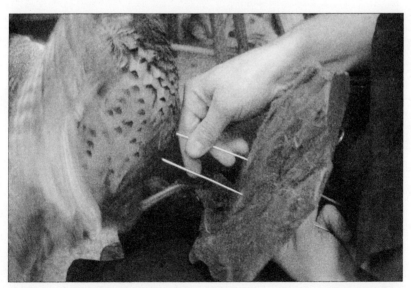

Anchor the wires in place by running a small screw back into the same hole from the underside of the base.

All species are attached using the same basic procedure. Drill holes in the base that are slightly larger than the attachment wires protruding from the mount, and then insert the wires and snug the bird up tight.

obtain from a taxidermy supplier. Where I live in the Southeast, most of the driftwood I find is very soft pine.

The procedures for attaching a flying or standing mount to a base are basically the same. I have discussed these steps in the chapters on mounting specific birds, but let's review them again here.

Start by drilling two appropriate-sized holes for the wire exiting the feet (standing mount) or the body (flying mount). These holes should be only slightly larger than the wire. For standing birds, slide the wire through the holes and pull until the mount is firmly on the base. For flying mounts, don't pull the wire so tight that the wings touch the wall when the mount is in place.

When you have the wires as tight as you want them, screw small screws (about one inch long, depending on the thickness of your base) back through the holes from underneath to lock the wires in place. Then cut off or break the wire level with the back of the driftwood. Depending on how clean a break you made on the wire end, you may want to cover the area with glue and felt or cloth. This will prevent the sharp tip from scratching furniture or the wall.

Base work can be much more elaborate than this, but driftwood is a good starting point for beginners who need to focus most of their attention on the mounting process. On later projects, you can add all types of natural and artificial materials to create a diorama to complement your mount.

CHAPTER 12

Tips for Achieving a Better Mount

CHOOSE THE CORRECT MANIKIN

Choosing the right manikin for your mount may seem elementary—and it should be. But it seems that many novices, and some trained taxidermists, just don't understand the importance of using an appropriately sized manikin. Think about it: everything that is taken out must be replaced with something of nearly identical size or problems will occur.

Unfortunately for the upland bird taxidermist, most makinins created for individual species are limited to only one or two sizes. This is because only the rare pheasant or grouse exceeds an "average" size, unless it happens to be raised domestically. So roughly 90 percent of the time commercially made manikins will fit your bird skin with only very minor adjustments. But if the manikin is too large, you'll have a heck of a time aligning the skin, and it won't matter how meticulously you followed the other steps in the mounting process.

Several taxidermy suppliers and sculptors offer manikins, and if you do more than one project you will soon have a favorite. Taxidermists just seem to be more comfortable working with forms they are used to and have confidence in. If there are no commercial manikins available for a particular project you will probably have to wrap or carve your own body.

REPAIRING BENT OR BROKEN FEATHERS

Bent or broken feathers occur all too frequently. Whether from the shot, a retrieve by a hard-mouthed dog, or careless placement in the freezer, damage is sometimes unavoidable. Take every possible precaution and then repair what you must. Of course, some areas are more easily repaired than others.

Any feather damage can be detrimental to a mount, but the most noticeable problem areas on upland birds are the back feathers and the wing primaries. Hopefully, you will only have to deal with one or two of these, and it may be possible to hide the damage with the right pose. For example, when a pheasant has several broken primary wing feathers, it is best to mount the bird in a standing position. A flying position would only call attention to the damaged area, but by closing the wings you can usually keep the problem well hidden.

If a bird happens to have damaged scapulars (shoulder feathers) you may be able to mount it with both wings up. This forces the scapulars together slightly, which makes any problems less noticeable. Severely damaged areas are always difficult to hide. And it may be impossible to do so. Only experience will tell you whether or not a skin is salvageable, but whenever possible it helps to first repair the damaged area.

In situations where a very special piece has been damaged—a child's first bird, a rare ruffed grouse color phase, a special hunt—the taxidermist must be more creative. A bird that has severe damage on an entire side may need to be placed in a closed habitat where the affected side can't be viewed. It may sound crazy, but a pheasant that has a severely damaged head could possibly be mounted lying on its back in a dead position to hide the damage. (I've actually had to use that pose.) Even if the body of a pheasant or quail is badly damaged you may be able to place it into tight cover arranged on the base so that the rest of the bird can't be seen directly. The possibilities are endless; it all depends on the specific situation.

The above examples are extreme, and in most cases repairing a damaged area is quite possible. To fix a wing primary, and this is possibly the most vulnerable area when the bird is in flight, you can either repair the feather, pluck and replace it, or simply remove it. It is probably easier to remove a primary before the skin dries, but I usually like to wait until after the mount is finished drying. If only one feather is damaged just pluck it before mounting, and then simply close the gap by rearranging the surrounding feathers. No one will ever notice. I wouldn't recommend removing more than two feathers on each side this way, though, as the mount will begin to look unbalanced.

If you wait until after the bird is dry, just pull the damaged feather out and replace it with an identical feather from another bird. Use Super Glue to lock the new feather into place. If you don't have access to a replacement feather your only alternative is to pluck the feather before the mounting process begins. Don't go overboard plucking and replacing feathers, though. All birds lose feathers and have unruly feathers from time to time. A few such feathers will only add character and authenticity to your mount.

Freezer burn is another problem that seems to affect upland birds on occasion. This occurs most often in the foot, head, and neck areas. The body is fairly resistant to freezer burn, which I believe is due to the layer of fat beneath the skin and the insulation of the feathers. If freezer burn does happen, it will be obvious. The skin will be very dry and stiff, and the legs will be nearly impossible to move, even after thawing.

Luckily, the remedy is quick and easy. Just inject fluids into the freezer-burned areas with a small syringe. Inject a small quantity into various points, and then work the affected area around until it regains some mobility. Allow the bird to sit for a few minutes so the moisture has time to further soak into the skin.

There will be times when putting together a mount worthy of display seems all but impossible, but with enough patience you can save a lot of birds.

Properly Degrease, Clean, and Dry the Skin

These aspects have been covered thoroughly in the chapters on field care, skinning, and fleshing and degreasing, but their importance can't be stressed enough. You will quickly find that many problems can be reduced or eliminated completely by careful attention to detail in these areas.

Bring the Mount to Life

Correct head and neck positioning can breathe life into what would otherwise be an average mount. Most new taxidermists are hesitant to put much movement into their birds. They often just want to get a project together as soon as possible. This is fine initially, but after a few successful mounts you should really start to focus on creating lifelike poses.

The easiest mistake to make is mounting a bird with a straight neck and head or with legs that appear abnormally straight or rigid. A mount that portrays movement can be very convincing to an onlooker. Don't be afraid to put some bend into the head and neck area. The same goes for any portion of the body that can be moved naturally.

I recently saw good examples of the importance of perceived movement at a regional taxidermy competition. One display showed a pheasant in a cornfield, walking bent over while searching for kernels of corn. Another showed a grouse fleeing the clutches of an attacking bobcat. The legs were hanging down slightly as if the grouse had just flushed from cover and hadn't retracted his landing gear yet. The grouse's head was craned slightly to one side so he could see his attacker, and the wings were aggressively beating the air. Both these mounts were very convincing. The subtle bends that create the illusion of movement can change the whole look of a mount.

As you loosen up, learn more, and gain confidence you will eventually understand what it takes to re-create wildlife as naturally as possible. It doesn't happen overnight, but if you study the habits, attitudes, and personalities of a species carefully enough and long enough it will show up in your mounts in a host of subtle ways.

DRY THE FEET ON THE SURFACE WHERE THEY WILL BE PERMANENTLY ATTACHED

As you learn the art of taxidermy you will soon find yourself paying more attention to detail. I've touched on it throughout this book, but one detail that often seems to get overlooked by taxidermists is the attachment of the feet to a base. I hate to see an otherwise quality mount attached to a rounded rock or piece of driftwood with a completely open, flat foot. That's just not how a bird would stand. To achieve a natural look, which is always the goal, the feet should conform to the surface of the base.

If this problem occurs, it is because the taxidermist has allowed the bird's feet to dry on one surface and then attached them to another. To avoid this problem it is usually best to prepare the base *prior* to mounting. If you intend to make a final attachment of the bird to a truly flat surface you can usually get away with attaching the mount to a piece of plywood before drying. After drying, it can be moved to its permanent position. But if you plan to attach the bird to a log or a rock or anything without a perfectly flat surface, you should attach the bird to its final base while the feet are still flexible. Then tack each toe down securely while it dries. A bird with feet in this position looks natural. The feet actually appear to be gripping the surface.

CONFIDENCE

When I talk with other taxidermists, whether they are neo-phytes or veterans, I'm always struck by the fact that their biggest deficit isn't lack of knowledge but rather the lack of confidence. Confidence can make a big difference when you're trying to complete a difficult task. All taxidermists have gone through the same learning stages, the frustrations, the doubts. I can assure you that the taxidermist who wins next year's world, national, or even state championship is struggling to produce his best possible work. I can also assure you that his first attempt won't be remotely similar to the one that clinches the championship.

When the going gets tough and you feel like a project, or even taxidermy in general, isn't for you, just quit. But not for good. Take a short breather to gather your thoughts and get back in there. Things will get easier and your work will improve. And when it's all over you will feel the satisfaction of having completed something that took a great deal of effort and persistence.

JOIN YOUR STATE TAXIDERMY ASSOCIATION

Joining a state taxidermy association can really boost your learning curve. Taxidermy associations nationwide hold annual seminars and competitions geared toward improving the techniques and craftsmanship of their members.

Long ago, taxidermy was basically a secret art. No books were written, no videos shot, and you wouldn't have even thought of asking the taxidermist down the street for help. But times have changed, and joining a taxidermy association can put you a phone call away from the years of knowledge and experience of taxidermists in your area. Most taxidermists are happy to provide how-to instruction to a fellow club member. This is particularly true if they know you are new to the art.

The competitions are also a tremendous learning tool. Some of the best taxidermists in the world are often present to critique each mount that has been entered. This can be invaluable, because they usually offer tips on how you can improve your work.

SUBSCRIBE TO A TAXIDERMY MAGAZINE

Subscribing to publications like *Taxidermy Today* or *Breakthrough* can be a tremendous asset. Although they aren't geared solely toward upland bird taxidermy, there is usually at least a section devoted to birds in general or a specific species of upland bird. The articles detail some of the most advanced procedures available for taxidermists.

To subscribe to *Breakthrough*, call 1–800–783–7266. For *Taxidermy Today*, call 1–800–851–7955.

Index

skinning, 53
swollen appearance, 96

F
Fat tissue
  removal, 63
Feather(s)
  contaminants, 70
  contamination, 45
  grouse mounting, 117
  neck area, 68
  regulator needles, 104
  repairing, 148–150
  rinse, 69
Feather loss
  minimization, 11
  prevention, 9
Feather quills, 67
Feather tracts
  grouse mounting, 125
Feet
  artificial, 95
  attachment to base,
    151–152
  drying, 151–152
  finishing, 140–141, 141
  pheasant mounting, 106
Female bobwhite quail
  flying quail mounting,
    128
Field care, 5–12
  factors, 7
  freezer, 10
  guidelines, 12
  mounting, 6
Field dressing
  birds, 11
Finishing, 139–145
Fleshers, 27–29
  components, 27
  factory-built, 27

Fleshing, 59, 61–81
  breast section, 67
  knees, 48
  leg exposure, 67
  pheasant mounting, 106
  process, 28, 62
    completion, 72
    radius-ulna area, 88
  scissors, 63
  snips, 63
  systematic method, 66
  tail base, 65
  wheel, 61, 64, 66
    horsepower, 66
  wing bone exposure, 67
Flying bobwhite quail, 127
Flying mounts, 84
  attaching, 144
  leg reconstruction, 91
  leg wire, 89
  wings, 89
  wire insertion, 90
    photograph, 91
Flying pheasant mounting,
    105–116
Flying quail mounting,
    127–137
  anchoring, 128–129, 134
  body angles, 134
  breast, 129, 133
  delicacy, 127
  driftwood, 134
  eyelids, 132
  head, 132, 135
  legs, 129, 130, 137
  muscles, 130, 133
  neck, 135
  position, 134
  skin, 129, 130
  tail, 131, 136–137
  wing/body junction, 131